WHAT LAWYERS DON'T KNOW

How To Run a Business and Start Loving Life®

JEFFREY M. KIMMEL
& CONNIE HENRIQUEZ

Printed in the United State of America

First Printing 2020

First Edition 2020

10 9 8 7 6 5 4 3 2 1

ISBN: 978-1-7358865-0-3

This book is dedicated to all the open-minded self-starters out there seeking independence, power, and control over their lives. With the right tools and a positive mindset, you can achieve anything.

TABLE OF CONTENTS

JEFF INTRODUCTION

People think lawyers know everything. You know what I mean. At family gatherings, when any law-related topic comes up, everyone looks to you. Even if you're a personal injury lawyer, they want your expert legal opinion on why the President should or shouldn't release his tax returns. You went to law school, didn't you? What's the law? And with friends, it doesn't matter if you only practice criminal law, you're asked to "just look over" the lease agreement for your buddy's new office space. As a lawyer, you *must* know what's really important in any contract. It doesn't matter that you graduated law school last year or 25 years ago, *you're a lawyer*, aren't you?

The truth? There's a heck of a lot that lawyers don't know. The area of practice you choose (or that chooses you) becomes what you really know. Specialization has overtaken general practice "shingle-hangers." Many lawyers are one-trick-ponies. They know their area of law and not much else.

I think that's great. Clients benefit from highly trained and experienced lawyers managing their specific issues and needs. Nobody wants to be a lawyer's first case. Would you tell a client, "I've never tried a case before, but I'm really excited and ready to go on yours?"

The message for lawyers: Know what you know and know what you don't know. Just because *people* think you know everything about the law, *you* know you don't. Don't pretend you do. Don't guess at what your friend's business lease should say. Refer him to a lawyer who knows.

So, what is it that lawyers don't know but absolutely need to know? Here's a hint: It has nothing to do with the law. It has everything to do with the *business* of law. Has any family member or friend ever asked for your advice on how to run a business? Probably not. Did anyone ever ask you to interpret a financial statement or discuss a marketing strategy? Of course not! You went to law school, not business school.

Most lawyers have no clue how to run a business. That's ok. It's not your fault. You never learned how. It's not taught in law school. Your bosses never discussed it with you. You probably never asked anyone about it. You were hired to be a lawyer, not run a business. You've focused on the assignments given, the law related to your cases, communicating with clients, and making your bosses happy. The goal has been to get the work done efficiently and resolve the cases favorably.

But you, my dear reader, are not like most lawyers. You are different. You were intrigued by the title of this book. Maybe something happened in your life that opened your eyes to the business of law. The COVID-19 pandemic drove many lawyers onto the unemployment rolls, mostly for business-related reasons, not performance. That'll wake people up! Or perhaps you're one of the few entrepreneurial types who wants to run a business but isn't sure how. Or maybe you're currently running your business and you need some tips on doing it better. Even if you have zero intention of ever being the boss or running a practice, it is important to know how the business works. It will make you a better lawyer.

Running a business the right way, any business, starts with YOU. Success and happiness begin with you taking control over your MIND. Before you can run a business and lead anyone, you must have the confidence in yourself, a clear vision of your goals, and a positive outlook for your future. You must control your own mindset before you can motivate or manage yourself and anyone else.

How do I know this? Connie Henriquez, who is my everything (fiancée, partner, life coach, professional development consultant, quarantine-mate, best friend, confidant … you get the picture) changed my way of thinking.

She wrote this book with me, sharing her unique philosophies on life, business, love, and happiness.

That's how this book works. I provide the nuts and bolts of running a business and managing a firm. She teaches how to improve your mindset, achieve your goals, and Start Loving Life. I'll let her explain that …

Connie Introduction

So, you want a step-by-step instruction manual on how to create your own firm, run a business and Start Loving Life? A BIG CONGRATS to you! There has never been a better time to start planning your future. Why? Because you have more control over your life than you ever imagined. You always have; you just didn't realize it. Having this book in your hand itself is the greatest step towards loving life. Get ready to learn the fundamentals of true success by being your own boss and being truly happy! Together, we will explore the easy and simple steps to create the life you want AND deserve.

It's no coincidence that Jeff and I are writing our first book together during the COVID-19 health crisis. In times like these there are those who struggle and those who thrive. As a life coach, I always teach those who are opting for a better life. This book is for those who wish to thrive and seek a clear-cut plan. Although some principles here may need to be placed on hold due to the current economic and social restrictions, this book is about creating a long-term plan to build a solid foundation for you and your new RICH, FULFILLING, and HAPPY LIFE.

Don't be discouraged and don't be afraid. Your time to shine is now. It requires nothing more than opening your mind, reading this book, and taking the first step towards a new, wonderful life. Jeff and I are here for you, cheering you all along the way!

My portion of the book is dedicated to my hunnnnies, Jeff. He is my loveee and my partner, offering continued support and inspiration to teach the world how to Start Loving Life.

I am eager to share this book with you as it wonderfully combines our wealth of business experience and coaching expertise. We will inspire you to your BEST LIFE EVERRRR!!

Jeff Chapter One

EVERYTHING HAPPENS FOR A REASON

Become a partner! That was always my professional goal. In law school, that's all I heard: Work hard, get excellent grades, join a good firm, and become a partner. That's the path to success! What did it mean to "make partner?" More money! Beyond that, who cared? Managing Partner? What was that? Nobody mentioned that in law school. Partners split the profits and made more money. That's all that mattered.

After years of trying cases, building relationships, and bringing in business, my dream became reality. Equity partnership! Ownership! My two older partners started the firm decades before, building its reputation as one of the premiere personal injury firms in New York. I was young enough to be their son, but they recognized my potential and brought me in. One partner tried the big cases and the other partner managed the firm. I followed the footsteps of the trial guy.

Transition to partner was easy for me. My job and responsibilities didn't change. The managing partner oversaw the business. I had almost no involvement in running the firm. I kept my head down and continued doing what I always did: stay focused, work hard, try cases, and bring in business. I kept riding the wave!

And then it happened. Just when I thought I had it all figured out. Right when things looked smooth, comfortable, straight, and narrow, that's when Connie came crashing in!

From the start of our relationship, she provided a novel and completely different perspective on life and business. As a life coach, she created her own lifestyle brand, Start Loving Life®. Everything was positive.

Everything was great. Anything negative or bad was actually good. You just had to learn how to spin it.

Huh? My analytical and painstakingly factual way of thinking couldn't process this initially. Anything bad was really good? What the heck was she talking about? Initially, nothing made sense. She doesn't even watch the news or read the paper! How does she know what's going on? What world is she living in?

This "go-with-the-flow" attitude and rose-colored picture of life fascinated me. We started dating and I began learning (and I'm still learning). I had no idea how much my life would change for better and how her philosophy would impact me both personally and professionally.

Soon after we met, the firm's managing partner died. The remaining partners (including me) were essentially clueless as to the firm's management. We looked at each other and sort of shrugged. Nobody volunteered to assume that role.

Given my business education background (albeit almost 30 years prior), the job fell on me. Just like that, all my responsibilities completely changed. I was now running the firm! What did that mean? I had no idea. We had about 40 employees, mostly non-lawyers: full timers, part timers, outside consultants, a bookkeeper, accountant, file clerks, legal assistants, paralegals, per diem workers. What were their job descriptions? What did they do every day? Who did they report to? Who supervised who? Who was checking up on everyone? How was everyone using our case management software? Who reviews our bills? How did we pick these vendors? What happens when the copy machine jams and a computer screen freezes? What safeguards were in place to ensure we didn't commit malpractice? What were everyone's working hours? Who keeps track of everyone's vacation time? What benefits package was offered to the non-lawyers? What happens if someone comes in late? Did we have any rules?

Was anything written down anywhere? Was I responsible for all this? What about my cases? Who was going to work on my cases?

As Connie always says, there are no coincidences in life. Everything always happens in perfect timing. There's always a reason why things happen. Little did I know how true this would be.

Connie helped me embrace my new role in an extremely powerful way. She taught me that success without happiness is meaningless. Her messages: "Life is not about working hard but instead working smart," and "The more you focus on your own personal happiness, the more your life and business are impacted in a powerful, positive way."

She inspired me to be the leader in my own life, which led me to inspire those around me at work and everywhere else. I truly discovered my best self: happy, loving life and loving my job even more.

This book will inspire you! We want you to succeed! You deserve all the best life has to offer. With my practical advice and Connie's Start Loving Life philosophy, you will learn about the business of law, running a practice and even more importantly, you will discover the keys to success and happiness. Who doesn't want that?

Ok, folks. Fasten your seatbelts. Heeeeeere's Connie!!!

ESTABLISH THE MINDSET

FOR A MEANINGFUL CAREER AND LIFE

I'm not a lawyer!

I'm a life coach! But I do live with a lawyer and have been coaching lawyers for years on how to be successful in law AND in LIFE. How to Start Loving Life® is my specialty and the brand that I created to teach people what they don't learn in school. How to love life, but most importantly how to start loving themselves. I know, this may sound super-cheesy, especially with how most lawyers think, but this is actually the reason why it has been so effective in helping lawyers step up their A-game.

You see, by nature lawyers are typically super-analytical AND extra-hard on themselves. Somehow, in law school you create these crazy expectations of who and what you should be in order to succeed. Except what happens is you never really develop your true self. And as a result, you put some serious pressure on yourself which has been seen associated with the rise of stress, anxiety, and depression within the legal industry.

That's where I come in. I teach lawyers how to utilize their unique personalities and strengths, so they never fall victim to being someone they're not. Here's the lesson:

You are unique. *You* are your brand. You must learn how to leverage your brand (YOU) to create a life you love, both personally and professionally.

Anyone can do this. You just need to know how. That's what I explain in my portion of this book.

While Jeff wrote the first draft of this book, he asked for my thoughts. I loved it! I thought it was great, practical advice for lawyers, or anyone interested in creating their own business. But I tend to see things a bit differently from Jeff's logical, structured approach to (almost) everything. Shocking, I know. HA! So, with my input, we came up with a book that considers the objective, as well as the subjective part of a lawyer's life journey.

We are so excited to provide you with the necessary steps AND positive mindset to create a life YOU LOVE. A life where your confidence soars, your creativity kicks in, and you become unstoppable on your quest to professional success and personal happiness.

Do You Love Being A Lawyer?

I often ask this question first as I find most lawyers have never even contemplated whether they love what they do.

The reason why this is important is because this book is about helping you fulfill your true potential. Maybe it's being a lawyer because you love it. Or maybe it's realizing you don't love being a lawyer, and you should be doing something else. The good news is, there is no wrong answer. This book is about you AND your life. As you go through the information I provide, I want you to really think about what YOU want out of your life.

My goal is to offer insight to help you think in a different way, giving yourself permission to choose the life you want as opposed to the life you are living now. That is, being a happy lawyer or being happy doing something else with your law degree. You get to decide, and the business tools Jeff teaches, together with my life advice, will help you do just that.

Why You Must Love What You Do

Success in business starts with success in your life. If you're not waking up every day excited about your life, your job and what the future holds, then you are missing out BIG TIME!

Think about it … how many people do you know who are super happy and excited about their lives? I'm going to guess, not many. So many people settle for a career path that's just not right for them? How does that even happen? People make choices early on in life (because of youth, inexperience, family pressure, peer pressure, societal pressure, or just limited knowledge) and then fail to realize they have options to change them at any time.

I'm here to tell you that you DO have options. You always have options. You're allowed to change your mind. You're allowed to shift or change your career. You're allowed to follow your heart. You're allowed to go with the flow. You deserve to be happy!

I can hear many of you saying, "Wait, I have a family, a mortgage, car payments. How can I change my mind on work? I have responsibilities!" Ugh, the dreaded word: responsibility. Yes, of course you do. But let me tell you this, which I know you didn't hear growing up: Your first and primary responsibility is to *yourself.*

If you are not truly happy and dread every single day, I guarantee you are not as productive as you could be, not as loving to your family as you should be, and certainly not as loving to yourself as you MUST be. Instead, you are pretty miserable for choosing this career path, and your family and so-called responsibilities reflect that.

So, what's the answer? You may not be able to do a 360 right now in your career, BUT you can start planning for one. Meaning, if you are pursuing a career you can't stand, then you must start planning some steps for a change.

For example, start saving money as an "emergency fund" to aid you through a career change. Take classes or courses at night. Finish reading this book to empower you to become the person you were meant to be. You will finally have the confidence to feel great and decide what you want, whether it's law or something else. Either way, this book will empower you to make a decision.

The point of this is that every single person is meant to pursue his or her passion. When you do, you never work a day in your life because you love it. If that's not you, it is never too late to change your mind. The intention is that you realize this is your life and you must do what's right for you.

Creating a life and career that you love begins by respecting, appreciating, and loving YOU. That kind of self-awareness and confidence will launch you towards success in anything and everything. That's what I've been teaching my clients for years and it works.

How Will This Book Help You?

Jeff will review the actionable steps to building an efficient, prosperous law firm. He has made the process simple. You'll learn how to become the boss and create a business.

The wonderful thing about this book is that even if you're not a lawyer yet, or if you ever decide to change your mind about being a lawyer, this book will still help you. The lessons here are transferrable to most professions. Knowledge is power. Just knowing these simple steps helps understand business in general, something everyone should learn.

My comments come from a different angle, but they're essential to establishing a new powerful, positive mindset that will create a meaningful career and life. Equally important to learning the steps towards success is creating the mindset to attain that success. Many people are deemed "successful," but how many of those people are really, truly happy? Not many. You deserve both: happiness AND success! AND neither is based on your job title or income level. It's based on your own self-perception which equates to your personal brand (which you will learn more about later).

When you begin to believe in yourself, your whole life changes. Not because of the success you may or may not have achieved in the past, but rather by how you feel about yourself. Are you leveraging your uniqueness and personal strengths (Positive Mindset)? Or are you constantly being hard on yourself and comparing yourself to others (Negative Mindset)? Knowing the difference between these two mindsets is really a game-changer. Take it from me as I have worked and seen the transformation of many lawyers who followed this path.

Is this way considered unconventional? Of course! But, if you are reading this, you weren't meant to fit in. You were meant to stand out! Unconventional happy lives require unconventional methods. Don't be afraid of being who you were meant to be. Most people are, but that is not you. You are different.

That's why I'll be sharing easy, simple advice to help elevate your mindset to a new level. I encourage you to open your mind and start thinking a bit differently. A lot of what I teach will challenge much of what you were taught growing up. This is a good thing! I'm not looking to convince or persuade you to change. Just be open to the material that resonates with you and provides a deeper understanding of who you really are, which is the answer to everything you are looking for. Success AND happiness.

Ways Lawyers Hold Themselves Back From BIG SUCCESS

Your current self-perception is old news. Why? It is based on your past self. Your old self. The before your "Start Loving Life" self. How do I know? Because that's where everyone gets hung up and never realizes it. So, I'm going to share four BIG ways you have been holding yourself back, in order to propel you forward to the NEW YOU. Understanding and embracing these concepts will change how you feel and think, improve the decisions you make, and increase your potential for achieving more.

1.   Why You're Smarter Than You Think

I personally can't stand when I hear someone define a person as smart or not. That statement itself is not smart. And here's why:

You are SMART. Embracing *everything* about yourself is SMART. All of it. The good, the bad, and the (so-called) ugly. It's you finally understanding that you were meant to be the real you, *whatever that looks like for you*. When you finally start to OWN your unique style, personality, and strengths, you are NO LONGER limited by the hold society has placed on you, starting from when you were young.

That's what makes you "smart." Why? Because when you fully develop and embrace the real you, you excel in ways like you never have before. It's as if your smartness is off the charts just for being you. You feel better about yourself, it's more natural to you, you stop second-guessing what to say and how to act. You actually end up liking yourself. Imagine that? You like yourself so much, you no longer twist yourself into a pretzel trying to be what other people expect of you (exhausting!). Instead, you become the only person you were meant to be, you. Happy, funny and "you" smart.

Why is this important? Because MOST PEOPLE aren't their true versions of themselves. Most people come from a place of fear and low self-esteem. They drive themselves nuts wanting to be well-liked and accepted (you know … the people pleasers). It's because of these fears and worries (instilled since childhood) that most people are too scared to be who they are. So instead, they pretend to be someone they are not, in hopes to fit in. But then, they never stand out. How lame is that? They think they are doing themselves a favor but have no clue how they are hurting themselves AND limiting their TRUE potential.

2. Your School Grades Don't Make You Smart

Did you know most people start to define their intelligence at age 6? That's right, age 6! What the heck do we even know at age 6? The truth is every person develops differently at every age. Some at rapid speed, medium speed, or their own speed. I personally love the last one: their own speed. God forbid we encourage that!

Somehow, we set these crazy benchmarks as to where each kid should be and when. And if for any reason a kid doesn't fall within that benchmark … uh, oh! … something must be wrong. Let's slap a label on that kid, put him in those "special" classes and slowly kill his shot at knowing his true worthiness!

"Oh, but we're just trying to help him," say the teachers and school administrators. Really? I say they're just training him to be like all the other little followers who are taught that their intelligence is based on grades. The grades of Science, English, Math … blah, blah blah. Yet, none of those classes cover the development of YOU. What YOU are good at. What YOU love. What interests YOU. Nope. None of it.

The mainstream message is: If you want any hope of succeeding in this society and convincing people that you're smart, then you better conform to this nutty system and get good grades! Study your little brain out in every subject regardless of whether you like it or not.

When in reality …

Growing up, your worst subjects were nothing more than subjects in which you had no interest. If you did, you'd have been eager to learn them. Guess what? Not having an interest in a subject isn't a bad thing! You aren't meant to LOVE and excel at everything. Can you imagine? If you were, you wouldn't know how to spend your time or choose a career you enjoy. Hello? I'm sure you never heard *that* before.

Instead, you unknowingly felt bad because maybe you weren't great at EVERY SUBJECT. That way of thinking prevented you from discovering your own, unique, TRUE AMAZINGNESS.

Now, let's say you were one of those kids who forcefully excelled at every subject. Not because you thoroughly enjoyed every subject, but because your parents, teachers, coaches, friends, and even you defined your intelligence that way. That's what you had to do. And that's what you did. Instead of validating your existence by how you felt by embracing your uniqueness, you were constantly in a state of proving yourself, comparing yourself to others, competing with others to be the best, and using your grades or accolades to measure you as a person or as a good student.

In essence, you allowed your grades to influence how you felt about yourself. If your grades were good, you felt good and proud. If your grades were not good, you felt disappointed, frustrated, and used it as evidence that good grades equal feeling good and bad grades equal feeling bad.

With that type of training and mindset, you drive yourself nuts. Believing that only good grades equate to feeling good which equates to self-esteem is literally setting yourself up for failure. How could you possibly enjoy and excel in every subject?

The grading system for these completely random courses is simply not a measure of your intelligence. All that stuff is nonsense. Instead of motivating you in a purposeful way, that system creates self-doubt about whether you can maintain successes (good grades) and feel good. That's where the stress, anxiety, and dreaded perfectionism bug kicks in. You place undue pressure on yourself to perform as if your happiness depends on it, because according to you (and everyone else) it does!

It actually doesn't. *Your happiness comes from understanding you.* What makes you, you. Accepting your uniqueness, your differences and being proud of the person you currently are, AND the person you are becoming.

It's your own self-perception. That's it. Happiness is an inside job and has NOTHING to do with anything outside yourself (unless you let it!).

3.   Failing Is Good And NECESSARY!

The system also taught you to steer clear of any type of failure! God forbid you put yourself in a position where you couldn't be the best. That would be sheer torture. So, you learned to avoid things, not because you were afraid to try but because you became accustomed to fearing failure. You eliminated putting yourself in situations where you could be criticized or not applauded. Simply put, you learned to validate yourself by other people's approval of you (friends, parents, coaches, and teachers).

Newsflash: *To be successful in life you MUST FAIL.* You must fail A LOT. And you must be so confident in yourself that you begin to realize if you aren't failing, you aren't trying. That's where confidence comes from.

Failing is NOT a result of a mistake you make. Failing is being SO confident in yourself that you are willing to TRY ANYTHING to improve yourself and your life. Be proud of all the moments you "fail" because those allow you to refine the process and perhaps redefine what you want. Only the courageous rise up again. Simply ignore anyone who criticizes your failures. I can almost guarantee that the critics haven't done much with their lives. That's why they are quick to judge yours (ouch! I know).

The most successful (honest speaking) people will admit that their path to success always included a bunch of so-called "failures" along the way. But not in an embarrassed way. In a proud, "I-believed-in-myself" kind of way. If you want a BIG LIFE you must be proud of your good, bad and (so-called) ugly. Why? Because in this lifetime YOU are all you got.

Notice, I didn't mention your spouse, partner, kids, or parents. Nope. That's on purpose. In this life, you have control over one person and one person only. You. Which means in order to be truly happy (which you are meant to be) you must become your own BIGGEST FAN and

CHEERLEADER. Of course, not in a conceited way. But in a "I-love-myself-so-much," and "my-life-has-become-so-good" way, that you want to be the inspiration for others to do the same for themselves! This is the avenue to everyone's happiness!

4.   Why Your Negative Self-Talk Matters

Negative, critical, internal self-thoughts are the ABSOLUTE worst emotions any person can ever feel. Yet, we do it all day, every day without even realizing it. We are so quick to make judgments about ourselves for all the ways we aren't living OR for all the things we could have done better.

You must stop thinking that way. This kills your confidence and your potential to succeed. *You cannot access your true potential if you are constantly holding yourself back mentally.* That is why you must be kind to yourself in your mind. Talk to yourself as you would to your closest relative or friend. Be easy on yourself and be proud of yourself for anything and everything. Not by measuring what you have achieved or by what you have, but AGAIN by how you feel about you.

When you learn to like "you" regardless of anything outside yourself (just because) you will no longer give a rip about what anyone thinks of you. And why is that good, you may ask? Because the only opinion of you that matters is your own. And when you finally realize the power is within you, by LIKING you and BELIEVING in yourself, you will no longer seek other's approval or validation to be the person you were meant to be.

(Insert mike drop and loud cheer here!)

Jeff Chapter Two

CREATE A NICHE

Whoa! Looks like you just got Connied! Lots of new thoughts and perspectives in there. I'm sure there were a few, "wait a second … what?" moments for you. Been there. Just go with it for now. It will soon make a lot of sense.

Michael Jordan Gets It

I just finished watching The Last Dance – the Michael Jordan documentary that provided a welcome distraction for millions during this pandemic. One segment had me thinking his Airness was a Start Loving Lifer (that's what Connie's followers call themselves). It had nothing to do with basketball but everything to do with his mindset.

In the midst of Jordan's ultra-fame during the 90's, a liberal African American Democrat (Harvey Gantt) looked to unseat the longstanding incumbent Republican U.S. Senator from North Carolina, Jessie Helms. Jordan refused to publicly endorse Gantt and famously commented that, "Republicans buy sneakers, too," setting off a firestorm of anger and disappointment within the black community. His reason? "I wasn't a politician. I was playing my sport. I was focused on my craft. Was that selfish? Probably. But that was my energy."

He didn't care what other people thought. He wasn't bound by expectations others set for him. He believed in himself and did what felt right to him. He was a basketball player. That was his niche and his specialty. That's what he loved to do. He wasn't seeking approval from anyone besides himself.

Those benchmarks and standards created by the black community didn't deter him from being his true self. He explained, "It's never going to be enough for everybody … because everybody has a preconceived notion of what I should and what I shouldn't do … The way I go about my life is I set examples. If it inspires you, great … if it doesn't then maybe I'm not the person you should be following."

Look at that! He even delivered the message. If you don't like who I am, don't follow me. Go follow someone else. Or better yet just follow yourself. If you believe in who you are and what you can do, you don't need to follow anyone.

Back To The Law

Here's what I love most about the legal field: Its reach in our society is endless. It encompasses, on some level, almost every business imaginable. Areas as diverse as corporate, litigation, environmental, patent, matrimonial, immigration, politics, criminal, transactional, real estate, entertainment, wills, trusts, guardianships, etc. all have lawyers. The list goes on and even continues to expand. COVID-19 has spawned new thinking and innovative areas for lawyers to explore. Even in a changed world, lawyers are critical.

When I first graduated law school, I interviewed with several "general practitioners." I marveled at how they could know so much about so many different fields. How did they learn all this? Was it as simple as having the right research material? Just look it up and you'll find the answer? (This was before you could ask Google or Siri anything). I had some basic understanding of a few concepts, but no knowledge on the practical application of anything!

General Practitioner vs. Specialist

No offense to the "general practitioners," but what does that term even mean to a potential client? What the heck is a "practitioner?" What do people think you do? And who wants to be known as a "general" anything (except maybe in the military)? How do you differentiate yourself? How does anyone think to call you when they need a lawyer?

Here's the paradox I've found with clients and their needs:

On one hand, most people think every lawyer can do anything law related. Most don't know the difference between lawyers who do personal injury vs. matrimonial law vs. bankruptcy vs. trust and estates vs. corporate law. Not because they're ignorant, but because they don't want to know until they need to know. To most people, lawyers are lawyers.

The average person thinks that way about doctors, too. All the medical specialty fields are complicated with weird names. Who knows what an otolaryngologist does? You probably don't, unless you needed to visit someone for your ear, nose, or throat problem.

However, as soon as someone *needs* a lawyer, they want one who handles that exact kind of case almost exclusively! They're looking for the best attorney *for their issue*. If you handle any other types of cases, it dilutes your experience for their case. The Ford dealership doesn't sell Toyotas or Hondas. At the Ford dealership, you only choose from Fords!

How do you please everyone? You don't. You have to find your niche and then own it.

Find That Niche

Ethically, lawyers are prohibited from using the terms "specialist" or "expert" to describe their practices (this stems from the fact that any lawyer can practice in any area without being certified to do so). Nonetheless, I've learned the importance of positioning a business and targeting a practice area to something specific: finding a niche.

My view is that the law is too complex for a "general practitioner" firm to be an effective business model. Clients want specialization that separates you from the tremendous competition in the legal world. Surely, there is something about you for you to build upon to set yourself apart from other attorneys. Not necessarily something new, but something different or something at which you can excel. Something with which you can find passion.

If you find yourself gravitating to a particular area of law, don't fight it. Go with it. Do you love music? The music industry has tons of lawyers! Are you interested in real estate? Real estate lawyers are everywhere! Attracted to the separate worldliness of bankruptcy court? People and businesses go bankrupt all the time! Pandemics and stay-at-home orders are great for their businesses. Excited by criminal work? There's plenty out there!

The more specific your practice, the less firms to compete with for potential clients, and the harder for competitors to duplicate your style and strategy. Having a niche enables you to speak directly to your ideal client. This targeted communication helps you attract people into your firm. Without a niche, you don't stand out and you're not speaking to an ideal client.

Hey, law students. Good news! School curriculums are getting better. Internship and externship programs are growing in popularity and are now required in many schools. Those can help you find your niche. Even if the experience doesn't particularly move you, eliminating a potential practice area from your future is just as important as finding a potential one. But these programs aren't enough. The experiences, even for a semester or two, are limited. The work assigned is, generally, superficial. And students are never exposed to the *business* of the law firm. Nobody pays attention to this!!!

Get Creative

Your niche doesn't necessarily need to be in a particular practice area. It may be a community to which you can relate. New York City, for example, is a melting pot of international communities, which tend to group together geographically. Many of these communities look within for recommendations for goods and services, including legal needs.

If you speak the language of a particular community, or have staff that does, that could be a beautiful inroad to connecting and meeting their legal needs. Language barriers affect relationships. I never feel great about convincing someone I'm the lawyer for them through an interpreter.

For the kind of law I practice, I need to form a personal bond and trust with the client. For most cases I handle, we enter into a long-term relationship. We need to connect. We both need to be confident that we're right for each other. With an interpreter bridging that conversation, there's always something lost in the translation.

Bonus: Being able to communicate in a meaningful way with a community may be your niche. If so, exploit it! Use those language skills to grow your business!

My advice: Find the area of law you were MEANT to practice. Gravitate to what comes easy and naturally. Make that your niche!

Back to Connie ….

CLARITY IS KEY

You Need Clarity

My philosophy offers you new insight and most of all, clarity. Clarity is important because the more you understand who you are and what you ideally want out of life, the more meaningful your decisions and sense of focus becomes.

You won't continue to mindlessly go to work every day in routine. Instead, you'll wake up every day super-charged and excited, with a clear goal ahead of you, knowing everything you want is in fact attainable. You will no longer play small in fear of the unknown. We're here to help you reveal the "known" in your mind, which is the first step in preparing the life you are about to lead.

Every crappy job you ever had (or have) was a godsend. I wish I learned this earlier when I was stuck in a job I didn't like. Each of those crappy jobs taught you something. If the job wasn't for you, you learned what you *don't* want to do. If you had a horrible boss, you learned how to (or how not to) deal with a bad boss. If your work environment was terrible or the office culture was toxic, you learned what to look for in the next job.

Learning from these experiences benefits your future. Unfortunately, so many people downgrade past experiences and never see the bright side of what they've learned. You need to flip every negative past experience and use it to your advantage – something good ALWAYS comes out of something bad. Always. You just need to see it.

That was me until I started learning the law of the mind. Your mindset is everything. Most people go their entire lives and never learn that, which is interesting since the laws of the mind aren't new and in fact have been known to the most successful and famous people for centuries. Yet this simple concept fails to receive the credit it deserves, which is unfortunate.

If people understood how easy, simple, and fun life could be, the world would improve in a heartbeat. But for some reason, this stuff isn't mainstream. So, consider yourself lucky to be learning this material! And please take this stuff and RUN with it! You'll get the edge you're looking for. Trust me.

The Riches Are In The Niches, People!

Let me save you years of heartache and unnecessary wasted time: If you are speaking to everyone, you are speaking to no one. I wish I can take credit for that line, but I can't. It's in about every single business book and it rings TRUE every single time.

For lawyers, simply launching a general practice website (the modern version of hanging a shingle), creating a home page with some cheesy stock legal photos (the courthouse steps, wow), listing 20 different practice-areas in drop-down tabs, throwing in some SEO buzzwords, and waiting for clients to come running may sound good. But it isn't going to make you rich! If you try to cater everyone, you cater to no one.

Early on in my coaching business I targeted "everyone." I thought that if I specialized, I would be leaving tons of money on the table. Guess what? I couldn't have been more wrong. Yet, I see lawyers do it ALL THE TIME.

Why Is Picking A Niche SO IMPORTANT?

Simple: It positions you as an expert. Hello? Who doesn't want to be considered an expert in their field? Oh, that's right, all the store fronts that simply say "Abogado" (insert sly chuckle here).

As you position yourself as an expert and gain momentum, you differentiate yourself from ALL the "Abogados" (insert "freakish" sly chuckle AGAIN). THEN you will grow your practice to include other areas of law. Because as an expert you will create a community of clients that trust and look at you as "their" lawyer. That's when you can farm those cases out and make loot on those referral fees (another book, another time ... I digress).

How Do You Discover Your Niche?

It's easy. Like Jeff said, pick an area of practice you absolutely loveeeee. Why? Because first and foremost, the goal is to love your life. When you focus on an area of the law you love, you will enjoy your profession so much more! Plus, there are sooooo many areas of the legal industry that could benefit you in your personal AND professional life. How to choose? Just be honest with yourself and your feelings and pick an area that comes easy to you.

So many people think (wrongly) that unless there's a struggle in something, there's no reward. That's nonsense! The opposite is true. Pick an area that doesn't feel like work. One that just comes naturally. People who love their jobs say they've never worked a day in their life. That's true and that's what you want!

And remember, you can't get it wrong. Just pick a niche and try it out. But be open. The wonderful thing about choosing a niche is that *you're* making the decision about what you want to focus on. Not your boss, parents, teachers, family, or friends. Once you make this decision, you then spend your time wisely on driving that specialty, as opposed to wasting your time trying to do everything to please everyone else but yourself.

What do I mean by being "open?" Let's say you decide your niche and move forward in that direction, but it doesn't work. Maybe you come to realize that there's a different, better niche for you. Great! But you can't discover that until you make the initial decision and choice of a niche. The sooner, the better.

The ability to be "open" allows you to evolve. There's no shame in changing your mind or shifting your focus. Choosing one niche may very well be the path you need to reveal your ultimate niche. The original choice can become another past experience from which you learn and benefit. See that? Always the positive spin!

For example: Let's say your parents got a divorce when you were a teenager. As a result, you became familiar with some matrimonial issues. When you went to law school, you took a few matrimonial classes and rocked them. It was easy! You then got your law degree, read this book, became inspired, and decided, "matrimonial law is my niche." Well done!

So now, you're working at a matrimonial firm and it feels good. You're soon assigned a few cases where the clients need to liquidate assets and sell common property. This forces you to research some real estate issues. Suddenly, you start loving this real estate stuff. You realize there's tons of value in real estate. Lots of money to be made. And those clients aren't fighting about visitation rights, splitting retirement accounts, the cost of organic blueberries for a gluten-free child, or who gets the dog. Maybe this excites you. Is this niche better for you? Maybe. But then again, maybe this experience re-affirms your love of matrimonial law. Maybe it confirms that you're helping those making a drastic change in their lives. Maybe you love being the catalyst to help people separate in the fairest way possible.

There's no right answer. Only you would know. That's why it's so important to stay open. Changing your niche is totally fine. Once you decide and move forward in your niche, other ideas and opportunities will surely follow.

Some may disagree with this thinking. Like the "Abogados" (I can't help myself here). But just to reiterate, when you create a niche, you automatically position yourself as an expert in that field. It's called instant credibility! It doesn't mean you don't know anything else or that you only do one thing. But being an "authority" in one thing is wayyyy more powerful than being just "good" at everything.

Plus, your niche puts you on the map. Without a niche, you're not even on the map. Once that niche puts you on the map, you differentiate yourself from everyone. This "map" is your reputation in the field. After establishing a niche, you can easily transition yourself to other areas because people already know you.

Again, there is no right or wrong. Only you know what floats your boat. Just one caveat, do what you love and what you find most satisfying. Don't do something that you *think* will be a trend or because you *think* it's what's needed. Your heart will never be in it and you won't be fully invested. You must pursue what you *are* passionate about.

Remember: This is your decision. Don't listen to the peanut gallery of friends or family and what they think you should do. Only you know what's best for you. And like I said, it will evolve, just remain open!

JEFF CHAPTER THREE

GETTING BUSINESS – NETWORK!

Now that you've found an area you love, created a niche and you're loving what you do, how do you get clients? The real answer is, if you've found that niche and you love what you do, the clients will come. Maybe that's not the answer you expected, but it's true.

How do you get business? The standard answer is that you must *network*. I hesitate to use the word "network" because it's such a formal term. In fact, the best "networkers" are those who don't even know they're networking. You don't decide during your morning shower, "I think I'll network today." It's something that just happens.

Understand this: If you are seriously considering starting or growing your business, you must be resigned to the fact that *you* are the business. If you don't sell yourself, then nobody will. If you don't bring in the clients, the business will fail. When you start a business, you know this better than anybody.

Of course, it's helpful to join Bar Associations, attend social functions, become active in churches and temples, join political clubs, join social clubs, and simply get involved in the legal field and your local community. But if you're passionate about your work, that becomes evident at all these events and functions. People sense that you're happy in what you do; and people associate happiness with success. That's because happiness equals success (just ask Connie)!

It Starts In Law School

Hey, law students! Are they teaching you networking in law school? Anybody? Anyone? No hands up? Check the course offerings. Anything on how to network? What do I hear: silence? But guess what? *Law school* itself is your first and most important lesson in networking. What am I talking about? I'm talking about my personal experience and my favorite topic when I lecture to law students.

I entered law school straight out of college. No gap year. No real, full time work experience between college and law school. I was a professional student! I knew the student drill: Sign up for the right class, get the syllabus, go to class, take great notes, do the homework, memorize everything the professor said and regurgitate it all back on the exams. I had it down! I was ready.

My goal entering law school? Be in the top 10% of my class. Why? Only the top 10% got the big jobs after graduation. That was the only way to ensure the highest salary and the most prestige. It was all about the grades. I needed to get good grades. No, scratch that ... great grades! The best grades! I was focused.

I was so focused, that I viewed everyone around me, all my bright, shiny, scared, and eager new law school classmates, as barriers to achieving my goal. They were in my way! I needed to trample over 90% of these people to reach the promised land. They were the competition. The enemy! I would do everything possible to beat them.

Study groups? The heck with that. Why would I share my knowledge with anyone? Collaborative research? Are you kidding me? Why help them find a case that helps me? This was "Intro to Combat 101," people! Go out to lunch with them between classes? Did George Washington's troops have lunch with the British soldiers between Revolutionary War battles? I purposely rented an apartment around the block from the school, just so I could eat lunch at home, alone, and study! By myself!

Sadly, I'm not exaggerating too much. And the irony? I did get the grades. After my second year, I got the big summer job at the "white shoe" New

York firm paying the mega bucks in the big city. I joined over 20 summer associates who were told by a partner that we'd have to "steal furniture" to not receive a full time offer at summer's end. What happened? Four weeks into the program, the stock market tanked, igniting a huge recession. Only 4 of the 20 people received full time offers. I wasn't one of them. On my last day, I stole a desk lamp from a small conference room (I still have it).

It's All About Relationships

Here's the point, law students: The *relationships* you form with your fellow classmates during law school are worth much more than any class you take, any concept you learn or any grade you receive. Please read that sentence again. One more time, slower. Thank you.

Business is about relationships. Networking is about connecting with people. When you finish law school, the most important things you leave with are the relationships you've formed with the people you've met, including your professors (most of whom are wonderful and helpful). Whatever courses you've taken, textbooks you've read or statutes you've learned are almost meaningless.

I don't mean to minimize the educational experience, but whatever field you ultimately choose will require a much deeper understanding than anything you've learned in law school – trust me, you'll learn it! But the relationships you form, the experiences you share and friendships you develop will form the solid foundation of a social network that will continue to grow throughout your life.

And here's the best part – it's not hard! This is not something you need to strategically plan for. There's no studying involved. It's not something you need to memorize. All you need to do is be yourself! Be nice! Be friendly! Be open! Talk to people. Make friends. Mean it. Have fun. You don't have to like everyone, but don't exclude anyone. Gravitate to people with whom you connect. Embrace it.

When you graduate law school, you sail off into the deep, blue ocean of lawyers. Oh, joy! Starting a new job, meeting new lawyers, going to court, appearing before judges, making new deals, negotiating, arguing, compromising with adversaries … all of this can be intimidating. But what happens when you, a new attorney, attend a court conference and your adversary turns out to be a law school classmate? Relief! Hallelujah! "It's someone I know!" No need to fight! You catch up on all the "remember when" stuff and the "what's she doing now" nonsense. It's great. It's real. And it's easy.

And what happens when you attend that first social function at a Bar Association or some fundraiser your boss drags you to? After you show up (and head straight to the bar), you look around at the vast collection of suits, ties and heels, then check your watch to begin the countdown to the end of this torturous event. You grab a shrimp off the cocktail tray with your free hand. As you contemplate how to ditch the suddenly naked shell, out of the corner of your eye you spot a familiar face. A law school classmate! What's she doing? Checking her watch! What do you feel? Relief! Happiness! Someone to talk to! The conversation begins, you remember when and find out what she's doing now. Then she brings over her one of her fellow new associates, and you do the same and you're off and running. That's networking! That's how you get business! It's not going to happen every night but it's going to happen. Your classmates expand your network and you expand theirs. It's that easy!!!

Even a pandemic shouldn't stop you from networking. The legal field was slow to accept technological advancements before COVID-19. Not anymore! Attorneys, judges, and courts have been forced to sprint towards technology making everyone embrace a new normal utilizing Zoom, Skype and other platforms previously ignored by the profession. Video conferencing is not only a way to conduct court conferences and office meetings – it's another way to network. While it's all new now, it's going to get easier. Get ready for it!

Quick tip alert: Here's a suggestion for those with some experience looking to go solo: Start by doing per diem work. Court appearances, depositions, and court conferences are time consuming and sometimes inefficient use of an experienced lawyer's time. Offer your services to do these things (for a price). This allows you to network in several ways. It's an opportunity to show an experienced lawyer that you can do good work. Prepare detailed and thoughtful reports that accompany the bill for your services. You also achieve more "face time" in court, where you will meet judges and other attorneys. That's networking!

For those who are happy and passionate about what they do, the networking comes naturally. If those around you see that you're happy and doing well, more business will come your way. Everybody loves a winner. Everybody wants to be part of a winning team. Success breeds success. Networking is an art! It's not that hard. Just get out and do it!

It Has To Feel Right

I started this chapter by telling you that if you find your niche and you love what you do, the clients will come. I really do believe that. But more importantly, *you* must believe that. *You* must know that being true to yourself and having confidence in yourself is everything. You must accept that only when you align what you were *meant* to do with what you are actually doing, the riches will follow.

What does that even mean? Who do I think I am? Connie? Don't overthink it. Just be honest with yourself and how it feels. You know when you're doing something you don't like. Think about how uncomfortable and forced that feels. And the opposite is true: You know when you're in the zone, enjoying what you're doing, feeling powerful and being super-productive. Connect with those feelings. Recognize those feelings. Acknowledge those feelings. Act on those feelings.

I may be overstepping my bounds with this "alignment" and "feeling" stuff. I know I'm stepping into Connie's territory, but my point is that *you* are the business. When it's your firm, it's all about you. The way you carry yourself, the way you describe yourself, the words you use to explain the business, the confidence, energy, and genuine happiness you exude when talking about your business to anyone and everyone.

If all of that is sincere and honest, it will affect people in a positive way. Everyone loves a winner. Everyone wants to be part of a successful team. By the same token, if you're unhappy and complaining about how difficult your business is and how every day is a struggle, what's the perception here? Who in your life enjoys hearing a chronic complainer? Who would want to join that team? Who would want to hire that lawyer?

When it's *your* business, it's *your* reputation. As lawyers, we don't have much more than our reputations. And once a reputation is established, it's tough to change it. *You* make your reputation. Not just during business hours, but all day, every day. Do you belittle servers at restaurants when your order is wrong? Do you hold the door open for the person behind you entering the store? Do you compliment a stranger wearing a cool outfit? Do you thank your Uber driver for a great ride? Do you express appreciation to relatives who have your back? Are you a dependable friend?

Whatever your answers are to those questions, that's who you are. And that's the type of lawyer you should be. Just because you see lawyers screaming at each other in court doesn't mean *you* have to. If that's not you, don't do it. Being an advocate doesn't mean changing who you are. You can zealously represent clients without being a lunatic.

Forget the stereotypical lawyer portrayed in movies and TV shows. That's not real. You're real. Be real. Be who you are. If you're a calm, even-tempered, thoughtful person, then be a calm, even-tempered thoughtful lawyer. It'll feel right. And everyone around you will pick up and appreciate that. Your reputation should reflect who you really are. Only then, you can be truly comfortable and happy in your own skin. And that is when the business will flow, and the clients will come.

My advice: The word "networking" is the wrong term to describe all this. It shouldn't be thought of as "work" at all. It's being you. It's being yourself. That's not work. Talk with people the way you want people to talk to you. Treat people how you want to be treated. Care about people the way you want people to care about you. Just be you and the business will come.

BE THE BEST *YOU* EVERY DAY

Jeff is starting to sound a lot like me! Lol. Networking *is* easy. It's just you being you. But what does that really mean?

Consider this: You are a walking billboard. You represent YOU and your business every second of the day, whether you're working or not. It's not about being a so-called "good lawyer," whatever that means. It's about being a good person and loving and appreciating yourself (aka: not being hard on yourself). It's about taking pride in yourself and your contribution to the world at large. How you show up to your life every day plays a large role in how life works out for you.

How To Be The Best YOU Every Day

Do you treat yourself well? Are you nice to yourself? And I mean *mentally*. Are you appreciating all the great things about yourself or are you super-hard on yourself, constantly focused on what you just did wrong or what you could have done better?

Beating yourself up mentally like that affects and dictates your attitude every single day. If you do this, stop it right now! You're killing your confidence and limiting your true potential in every moment you are a jerk to yourself. Why would you EVER do that to yourself? There are plenty of obstacles outside of your control thrown in your path. Don't be one of them.

It's easy to be happy when things are great. That's a given. But we all know people who, as soon as things turn south, quickly become miserable and negative. Don't be *that person*. If your boss screams at you for making a mistake or demeans you in front of others, that's not your fault. That's simply your boss exhibiting his fears and worries in the moment and, unfortunately, it's directed at you. Perhaps your boss is having a bad day, or she is stressed about something unrelated to you. It's not a reflection of who you are.

YOU set the tone for who you are. If you treat yourself well, value yourself and know you're doing your best, that's all that matters. Granted, having a boss who acts like that sucks, but you can be above all of it by caring about yourself and doing your best to appreciate yourself (and by giving him a copy of this book-ha!). Bosses come and go. Some are good and some stink. But you're always the boss of your own mind. Be kind to yourself. Always give yourself the benefit of the doubt. It all starts in your head!

Your Morning Routine Affects Your Entire Day

How do you change your mindset? Make it a habit to start fresh every single morning when you wake up. You set the tone of the day by how you choose to start your day.

Think about it: Are you rushing every morning? Setting your alarm to the last possible minute, taking a quick shower, hustling through your routine? Are you timing the traffic, bus, or train to arrive one minute before 9:00? Yes? That means by the time you get to work, you're harried, overwhelmed, and stressed.

Try waking up a few minutes early with enough time to prepare for your day. Wouldn't that feel good? Wouldn't that make a big difference? Instead of grabbing your cell phone and checking e-mails as your first act of the day, how about reminding yourself of how lucky and thankful you are today. Take a minute to think of all the great things going on in your life, like the fact that you have a job. How about appreciating your health and your ability to get out of bed and be productive every day?

Give yourself a break. Take the time to list the qualities you love about yourself and what you appreciate about your life. Write them down on a piece of paper (or type them into a Note on your phone).

A Great Morning Exercise!

I'm not suggesting you write a book every morning. Just jot down a few thoughts about the wonderful "you." For example, write, "I am thankful for waking up healthy today." Exercises like this may seem weird at first. Most people are conditioned to please everyone but themselves. Too many people start their day with the news, which typically reports on everything gone *bad* in the world!

Creating a quick list about what you appreciate most about you simply puts your mind in the right place. Starting each day this way makes you feel good. When you feel good, your attitude is upbeat and positive. I guarantee that your reaction to the problems of the day will be more solution-oriented than if you were not feeling good.

Starting your day on the wrong foot, rushing to get out of the house, and not properly preparing your mind leaves you easily agitated. You get caught up in drama of the day and your problem-solving skills suffer. Why? Because when you don't feel good, it's difficult to allow effective solutions to flow in. Your mental well-being and attitude are paramount to your success.

What Does This Have To Do With Networking?

Even if you don't realize it, you're networking every minute of every day just by being you. In the office, you're selling your employees or subordinates on why they should do their jobs to the best of their abilities. You convey this through your words, actions, attitude, and how you treat them. You're selling your co-workers on why they should be open to helping you or supporting you by how you treat them. You're impressing your bosses with your "can-do" positive attitude and reminding them with words and actions why you're great at contributing to the firm's overall goals and philosophy. Everyone appreciates a positive attitude.

This is true outside the office, as well. At a restaurant for lunch? Your *attitude* is the business card you leave with the waiter, the establishment, and with the other dining guests. The same goes for networking events. Your *attitude* is what people see first. Did you walk in with confidence? Are you smiling? Making eye contact? Or are you too serious? Does your body language suggest openness or are you closed off? These things matter.

For those new to the social aspects of business networking, attending events can be awkward. It's definitely an adjustment for most people. Entering a ballroom full of strangers dressed in business attire who all seemingly know each other may appear intimidating at first.

You ask yourself: Where do I go? What should I drink? Should I stand or sit? What do I say? Why did I forget my business cards? Should I grab that stuffed mushroom with my fingers? Is there food in my teeth? Where are the toothpicks? Do I recognize that person from law school? What's her name again? Why isn't there any music? Why can't I remember her name? She sat next to me in Constitutional Law! Why can't I taste any alcohol in this drink? What time does this thing end?

All these questions are normal. Don't be hard on yourself. Don't expect to be a networking pro right out of the gate. There is a rhythm to working the room at these things. You'll get there. Just be open to trying new things every time you go.

Tips For Networking Events

Take notes of other people and what they're doing. Watch and listen to those who look relaxed and comfortable. What are they doing? Would that work for you? If not, that's ok. Find your comfort zone and stay in it.

Don't put undue stress on yourself to be perfect. Be proud of the little baby steps you make, even if that means smiling at the waitress or striking up a conversation with the bartender. You have to start somewhere! The more you do it, the more comfortable you will get.

Develop a strategy before you get there. For example, it's best to make a beeline straight to the bar as soon as you get there. No looking around or chitchatting until you have that drink in your hand. That's cool! You walk in with a purpose and a goal. I like that one.

What else? Set yourself up in a good spot where the appetizers are being passed. When you and a stranger both reach for the lamb chop, make a comment about the food. "I love lamb chops, but they're so messy." Start conversations about anything that comes natural to you. Comment approvingly on people's clothes (that's a great tie), the food, the weather, vacation plans, sports, movies, Netflix shows. Talk about what you love. You can always get around to talking business. Be a person first. Be yourself. Talk about what you know and enjoy.

WARNING: BE MINDFUL!

My pet peeve at these events is people who only talk about themselves! I can't tell you how many networking events Jeff and I attend where we get sucked into a conversation with someone who only talks about themself. These conversations are so NOT FUN.

We love to learn about other people and, in fact, we are thoroughly interested! Networking is about people getting to know each other. It's a back and forth. You're supposed to have pleasant, interesting conversations with people. It's not about lecturing others on your views of politics or the law. People don't want to hear long-winded stories about your last contract negotiation or trial. Listening to a one-way conversation is tortuous, boring, and makes for a great excuse to suddenly notice your empty glass and beeline right to the bar!

Don't be that person. Be open and inquisitive. Ask open-ended questions and listen to the answers. Have a genuine interest in the answers. Have a conversation! You may learn something. You may even end up liking the other person!

That's how you expand your circle. Exude confidence with your demeanor. Walk tall, be proud, smile, and be engaging. Look people in the eyes and pay attention to what they're saying.

Developing Your Brand: YOU

Whether you're at a networking event, your office, the courtroom, gym, grocery store or a Broadway show, your personal image is what people see and remember you by. Your attitude is a big part of this. But attitude aside, how do you represent yourself? How do you dress? Do you prefer conservative, stylish, fashionable, or flashy? Do you enjoy color? Bow ties? Custom suits? The first thing people notice is what you're wearing. What does your outfit say about you?

Don't go crazy with this stuff but do think about it. Develop a style that fits you and stick with it. This is, of course, a personal choice. You can choose to wear anything. But if want to stand out from the crowd, your attire, hair choice, shoes or any other outside accessories can add to your long-lasting business card of you.

The goal of "networking" is to embrace being you, have fun, and leave a lasting impression wherever you go. Again, only if you choose. If you prefer low key, that's cool too! If that's who you are and that's your comfort zone, then go for it and own it. Don't apologize for wearing your favorite black VAN sneakers to a fancy restaurant (Hi-that's me!). If that's who you are, then be proud and confident. Your attitude makes the outfit.

Live One Life

Your personal life must be consistent with your professional life. So often, people think that who they are at work should differ from who they are at home. I believed this for years when I worked for different companies in the cosmetics industry prior to my coaching life. But then, I realized: The more I was my upbeat, positive self at work, the more comfortable I became there and the more I enjoyed it. Moreover, my enjoyment led to results. I started to understand that by being me, I was more productive and encouraging to those who worked around me and for me. My attitude was contagious. I was being who I am, not who I was supposed to be. Who knew that the more I tapped into my true self and my personality, the more successful I'd be at work? That's what inspired me to leave the cosmetics industry and create a coaching business to teach people what took me forever to learn!

The same goes for you. If you're funny at home, be funny at work. If you're witty at home, be witty at work. Stop living separate lives. Live one life. I hate to break it to you, but you are one and the same person. Don't be different depending on where you are or who you are around. That is exhausting and NOT NATURAL for you. Be your one genuine self.

The more you embrace your true self at work without fear of judgment (you'll get over it – trust me) the easier it gets. You're always just you. That's really the road to happiness – when you realize your life is just a string of wonderful events, being the true you, whether it's at home or at work. That's what you want. It makes your life more enjoyable. You're less likely to begrudge working because it all becomes one and the same.

BIG TIP ALERT: Tell everyone what you do! Everyone! Sometimes we forget this and assume that our friends, family, and other business acquaintances already know (or don't even care) about the details of our work. Don't assume that! Talk about what you do and remind them that you're their go-to lawyer! Let them know you're available if they ever need assistance. Why? Because people give business to people they know and trust. That's you. But not everybody fully understands what you do or what your job entails.

As Jeff mentioned, there are so many different practice areas of law, but the reality is most people assume lawyers know something about every area of law. You can't change that. Just encourage people to trust you with whatever legal affairs they have or may have in the future. If it's an area of law you don't practice, it's a great opportunity for a referral: Call the person you just met at a networking event who practices in that field of law. That way, you're helping your friend or family member and getting credit for referring a case to your new contact. That's a great way to get a referral circle going.

Remember that all this networking stuff starts with you and your attitude. We all want to be happy. If happiness is your ultimate goal, you must address your own mental well-being first. When YOU feel good, you exude a different kind of energy than those who aren't caring for themselves and are stressed out and struggling. Your attitude is contagious, whether it's positive or negative. So be happy, have fun, and then TELL EVERYONE what you do.

JEFF CHAPTER FOUR

BASIC FINANCIALS

O k, people. It's time for some nitty gritty business stuff. Buckle up! This could be the scariest section for everyone. But it shouldn't be. Many lawyers claim they chose law school over business school because they "suck" at math (and eliminated medical school because they couldn't stomach seeing blood). Good news: You're allowed to use calculators in the real world. They really help!

Even though I graduated from the Wharton Business School, I left behind all my accounting, finance, and statistics knowledge once law school started. And for the ensuing 25 years, I never had any true "business" responsibilities in the jobs I held. During that time, I never even had a calculator in my desk drawer!

It was only when the Managing Partner in my firm passed away that I dove into the finances of my firm. Well, not exactly. For the first two years after his death, my other partners and I simply ignored the finances, figuring that "they would take care of themselves." We all deftly avoided the subject, letting the bookkeeper and accountant handle everything business related. It was not the best business approach for a multi-million-dollar firm! (And teetering dangerously into the realm of legal malpractice!).

Only when we exceeded our line of credit, maxed out our credit cards and faced a $100,000+ payroll, did reality set in. By default, and necessity, I then became the Managing Partner. Looking back, it was the best thing that could have happened to the firm and me.

I started by presenting the bookkeeper and accountant with a few questions. How much do we make? What do we pay everyone? What are our expenses? How much do we pay for all this stuff? *How much?* After some unsatisfying answers, I had a better question: Who's making all these decisions on spending? The answer? Crickets. (That wasn't an actual answer; it was the sound heard in the room when all went silent).

After my partner had passed, we were on autopilot. Our part-time bookkeeper was paying whatever bills she thought were necessary on any given day; she avoided paying larger bills by placing them at the bottom of a pile; we hadn't paid any estimated tax bills in over a year; but the partners continued to take our weekly draws and some percentage of the big settlements. Essentially, the firm was making a lot of money, but the business was rudderless and utterly inefficient.

Take Control

My first act as Managing Partner was mental. The first person I needed to speak with was me. I told myself to take control over what was happening. I needed to be the decision maker. I needed to know what was going on at every level of the firm. I realized the importance of breaking through that "fear of finances" and embracing this firm as my *business* that requires my attention, focus, thought, care, and nurturing.

Here's the point: It's *your* business. Nobody is going to care about it nearly as much as you do. Even your most trusted and loyal employees are limited in their ability to love the business as tenderly and wholeheartedly as you do. Only the owners of the business can view all the potential decisions from the proper perspective.

This may be a horrible analogy, but it's like dog owners picking up poop. If you love your dog, you may not enjoy picking up his poop, but you do it. Nevertheless, nobody else in the world feels that way about your dog's poop. You can hire a dog walker to pick it up, but that person will never feel the way you do about picking up that poop!

Profit/Loss sheet

Let's get into it. The most basic financial report you need to know is the Profit/Loss sheet. Hold on, now! Don't get dizzy. Don't get that glazed look in your eyes. Don't start skimming through the pages and check out the title of the next chapter. This is important.

But guess what? It's easy! It sounds intimidating but it is not. You're in business to make money; make a *profit*. If you're not making a profit, you're showing a *loss*. This sheet will tell you if the business is making money (profiting) or losing money (showing a loss). Simple!

If you have an accountant or bookkeeper, he or she can prepare it. If you don't, it's easy to prepare. It's simply a report that shows what money you've made (income) and what money you've spent (expenses). It itemizes these things according to your business.

It's a record of the firm's profitability for a specific period (a month, quarter, or year). There are two sections. The first section breaks down the money you've made (income), which for a law firm typically includes money from billable hours, either through hourly fees or fees paid in advance as part of a retainer agreement. For my firm, which works on a contingency basis, this number reflects the total amount of the money (legal fees) we've collected from our settled cases.

The second section breaks down the list of money we've spent (expenses), for things such as: salaries, rent, health insurance, malpractice insurance, office supplies, etc. That's it. That's all there is to it.

Here's a sample:

PROFIT/LOSS STATEMENT

Your Incredibly Successful Law Firm
2020
Income

INCOME

Fees from cases	$ 450,000.00
Fees from referrals	$ 50,000.00
Total Income	$ 500,000.00
Gross Profit (Loss)	$ 500,000.00

EXPENSES

Advertising	$ 50,000.00
Charitable Contributions	$ 25,000.00
Dues and Subscriptions	$ 20,000.00
Employee Benefits	$ 10,000.00
Insurance	$ 15,000.00
Interest	$ 2,500.00
Legal/Professional Fees	$ 5,000.00
Licenses and Fees	$ 2,500.00
Miscellaneous	$ 2,500.00
Office Expense	$ 30,000.00
Payroll Taxes	$ 5,000.00
Postage	$ 3,000.00
Rent	$ 5,000.00
Repairs/Maintenance	$ 7,500.00
Supplies	$ 10,000.00
Telephone	$ 20,000.00
Travel	$ 2,500.00
Utilities	$ 15,000.00
Vehicle Expenses	$ 7,500.00
Wages	$ 60,000.00
Total Expenses	$ 298,000.00
Net Ordinary Income	$ 202,000.00

OTHER INCOME

Interest Income	$ 5,000.00
Total Other Income	$ 5,000.00
Net Income (Loss)	**$ 207,000.00**

What do these numbers reveal? First, total up all the income. That gives you the sum of the money you've made for that time period. Next, total up all your expenses. That gives you the total sum of the money you've spent. Subtract the expenses total from the income total. If that's a positive number, congratulations! Bust out the cigars and champagne! You've made money! That's your net income.

If that's a negative number, you've lost money (a net loss). But don't worry if it's negative. Many new businesses start out with losses. And even with a loss, you and your partners may still have made money (if you've taken a draw or given yourself a salary throughout that period). With either outcome, the next step is the most important – analyze the details to find ways to get that net income higher!

How do you analyze these numbers? The easiest way is to compare all the current numbers to last year's numbers during the same period (month, quarter, or year). Are the current numbers higher or lower? It also helps to use percentages – what percentage has the number gone up or down?

You're simply looking for any big changes, up or down, that would signal a red-flag and require an explanation. For example, if your income in the first quarter (January through March) is up 25%, that's great, but why did that happen? What changed from last year's first quarter? Was it one big case or some efficiencies were improved? How can you keep that going up? What about if your advertising/marketing expenses are up 50%? How did that happen? Did you hire a marketing consultant to beef up your social media presence? Ok, that explains it. So, it is working? Is the consultant worth the cost? Is it too soon to tell? These are the type of questions to ask when reviewing the statement. When it's your money, you'd be surprised how quickly you catch on.

Good news: All this information can be kept electronically. An easy and popular program is QuickBooks. It spits out reports like this automatically.

For small business, there are many cheap options for this kind of bookkeeping program. Get one!

Accurately naming the expense categories is important. Be as specific as possible, so the data makes sense. In other words, instead of using "office expense" as a category, break the categories down into pens, paper, copy machine toner, etc. Instead of "outside consultant" be specific re: HR consultant, bookkeeper, appellate counsel, etc. Instead of "insurance," use malpractice insurance, health insurance, liability insurance, etc.

Income

The goal is to make money. Well, according to Connie, the goal is to be happy. Once you achieve happiness, the money will come. She's right, but let's talk about the money for now.

If the goal is to make money, set the goal. Make it real. Give it a number. Give yourself something to strive for. Set a target and hit it.

It's one thing to say, "I want to make a lot of money" or "I want to make as much money as I can." But what does that mean? Focus on a number, even if it's unrealistic. It motivates you. It gives you direction. It provides purpose. It works. What's the number? Whatever you want it to be. Look at last year's income. Want to double it? Triple it? Quadruple it? That's your number. Say it out loud. Put it out there. Simple.

Don't keep the goal to yourself. Let everyone in the firm know it. How can you expect your team to help achieve the goal if they don't know the goal? If you want your firm to gross $3 million, everyone should know that. What's more, everyone should be informed throughout the year how close you are to achieving that goal (or not). Quarterly updates should be provided to motivate the entire staff. Tie the employee bonuses to these goals. Create an incentivized system that puts everyone in the firm on the same page, with the same goals. You're all in this together!

Spending And Cash Flow

What happens when the money comes in? What do you do with the income? Buy a new car? Vacation? Shopping spree? Maybe, but what about the business? Some (if not most) of the money needs to be distributed throughout the business to keep it running.

Typically, the biggest expenses are payroll (if you have a staff), rent, and health insurance. And taxes! Never forget about the taxes! Regardless of your area of business, cash flow is an issue. You need cash every month to pay your expenses. But sometimes the cash isn't there. Sometimes the timing of the income isn't right, and you don't have the cash to meet these obligations. What to do?

I'll explain more on those issues, but for now let's focus on the cash. When the money comes in, you need foresight. You must view the big picture, know your expenses, and spread the wealth.

Here's what I do: My business is a contingency business. My cash comes in only after a settlement or favorable verdict – and not on the day of the settlement or verdict. There's a ton of paperwork to be completed (which takes time) and the insurance company cutting the check must run through its internal processes (which takes even more time). If I'm lucky, I get the check a month after the settlement date or verdict. It's typically even longer. If there's a child involved or if it's a death case, I need to obtain court approval for the settlement, which could take another six months or more! For those, I can't accurately predict when the money is coming in!

So how do I manage my cash flow? I created a "basket" system that took very little planning but a lot of discipline. For me, the biggest expenses are payroll and taxes. So, with every check received, I apportion a percentage to payroll (40%) and a percentage to taxes (30%). I created separate accounts in my bank labeled "payroll" and "taxes" to make it clear as day. When the bookkeeper deposits our share of the settlement money, she puts the designated portion into each of those accounts. This is not advanced accounting, people! The remainder is put into my "operating" account, which we use to pay our bills. Sounds easy, but when some of the bigger checks come in it's tempting to think, "why don't I just take this one home?" I've tried that. But when the firm became strapped for cash to make payroll one month later, I realized it wasn't worth it.

Expenses

"You need to spend money to make money." I'm not sure who told me that, but someone did. You can't start a business or grow one without expenses.

Everyone has a different relationship with money. Some people are cool with spending freely, while others fight to hold on to every last penny. Some combination of those is probably ideal, but either is fine. What's your relationship with money? Be honest! It's important to acknowledge, accept, and embrace that relationship if you're the boss making these decisions about money. The business should reflect whatever your relationship is; otherwise you won't feel comfortable making those decisions. Remember, the business is you and you are the business.

I feel better knowing that I "have a handle" on the expenses. We write way too many checks every day for me to know "exactly" what's going on. My comfort comes from analyzing the profit/loss sheet. The expense categories are broken down as much as possible. As mentioned, "office supplies" is too general. Being more specific and creating finer categories gives me greater insight into what we're spending money on. Reviewing these numbers and comparing them to prior periods reveals the trends up or down for each expense. Seeing that, forces me to think and be creative.

Last year, I noticed that the cost of paper doubled! After looking into it, I learned that we hired a new file clerk to help with trial preparation. We'd always done that, so why the increase? Well, the new file clerk was not instructed to double side all the copying for the trial notebooks. Problem solved!

Budgeting

My analysis of the expenses has led to BUDGETING, which is a great tool to rein in spending. We hired a terrify Public Relations consultant. She's modernized our website, beefed up our presence on all social media platforms and has us running around, attending worthwhile networking events and social functions. Everyone is now a "brand ambassador" to the firm! All good stuff, but it all costs money. Analyzing the numbers allowed me to come up with an annual budget for her.

The beauty of budgeting is that it removes the decision-making from your desk and places it elsewhere. That's music to my ears. Most of my days are spent answering questions and making decisions about money. I accept that and embrace it. But giving a department or an employee a budget makes it a once-a-year decision for me. "Here's $100,000 for the year, spend it wisely."

This shifts the responsibility to that department or person. More importantly, it makes them accountable for the spending. They'll use it as if it's their money. Otherwise, I'm constantly asked for money for different projects throughout the year. How about those "urgent requests" or "emergencies" where checks are needed immediately? I don't need that kind of stress. Let them figure it out. Then, explain to me what succeeded or didn't.

As owner, your personal compensation, whether it's a salary, draw or whatever, is also an expense that requires budgeting. That's a very personal decision, but it must be meaningfully and realistically contemplated and implemented in a reasonable way. Your personal needs versus the business needs must be balanced. It's just an exercise in prioritizing but be intentional about it. Don't let the business run you; you must run the business. That extends to all aspects, including money.

In my firm, the partners' compensation method has changed as the firm grew. Early on, when we had under 10 employees, it was easy for the partners to simply take big chunks from the big settlements. We had enough smaller cases to cover expenses and make payroll. At that time, we had a modest line of credit for cash flow crunches, but rarely dipped into it. All was good! But as we progressed, so did our expenses, especially payroll.

We grew to about 50 employees, with a fairly intimidating payroll. I implemented bi-monthly paychecks instead of weekly. That took some of the pressure off. Meeting payroll every two weeks instead of one gave us more time to get the cash we needed. In addition, the partners no longer rely solely on the big checks for income. Our expenses are so high; the firm needs most of that money to keep up with our obligations. Therefore, we instituted a bi-weekly draw that coincides with payroll and spreads out the payments. We still take money where we can get it, but now it's a lot more even and predictable.

It's all about the cash flow, people! If your business is more of a billing business, the income is more predictable, but you must still chase the clients to get those checks.

Escrow Accounts

Escrow accounts (trust accounts, IOLA accounts or IOLTA accounts) are the most important bank accounts for lawyers. You are required to closely monitor these accounts. That's actually the law. The account balance must be right. To the penny. Always. The vast majority of grievance committee disciplinary actions stem from irregularities with these accounts. What do I mean? Lawyers steal money from these accounts! Escrow accounts are where lawyers put other people's money. That's where settlement checks and real estate deposits are held until the money can be issued to anyone (the client, lawyer, bank, etc.).

The balance of this account often seems very large compared to your other accounts. Why? Because IT'S NOT YOUR MONEY! The disbarred attorneys found it very easy to take some of that money, thinking, "I'll just replace it before it's due." There is no real safeguard between you and that money besides your conscience (and the law). You can't do that. There should be better safeguards. That's why so many lawyers get criticized and disbarred!

Even though you may have a bookkeeper or accountant reconciling that account, you have SUPERVISORY responsibilities over that account: As a partner in the firm, you need to ask frequent questions and know what's going on.

I've avoided getting all citation-y and formal here, but I need to be a lawyer for a second: Under New York Disciplinary Rule (DR) 1-104(a), "A law firm shall make reasonable efforts to ensure that all lawyers in the firm conform to the disciplinary rules."

If you manage the firm, you have higher responsibilities because DR 1-104(B) provides, "A lawyer with management responsibility in the law firm or direct supervisory authority over another lawyer shall make reasonable efforts to ensure that the other lawyer conforms to the disciplinary rules."

One of those disciplinary rules is DR 1-104(C), which provides, "A law firm shall adequately supervise, as appropriate, the work of partners, associates, and non-lawyers who work at the firm. The degree of supervision required is that which is reasonable under the circumstances, taking into account factors such as the experience of the person whose work is being supervised, the amount of work involved in a particular matter, and the likelihood that ethical problems might arise in the course of working on the matter."

This point was underscored when a Long Island attorney was disbarred after he discovered his escrow account was compromised to the tune of $4 million. How? The bookkeeper, not an attorney, was funneling money from the escrow account. What made the case noteworthy was that the bookkeeper also happened to be the managing attorney's brother. The brother-bookkeeper was arrested, but the attorney was far from off the hook. The New York State Bar Association determined that the attorney (who turned in his brother) had violated ethical rules and suspended him.

Huh? Guess what went through my mind (and every Managing Partner's and sole practitioner's mind)? "Uh-oh." Did this mean that I now had to sit with the accountant, watch, and understand as he reconciled every transaction that went in and out of my escrow account? It sure sounded that way.

But it's not. Don't let that Long Island case scare you. Well, maybe you should, a little. You need to institute policies and practices to periodically review all your financials. Have your accountant and/or bookkeeper perform periodic and regular audits of the escrow account and report those results directly to you. Read the statements from the escrow account. Look over the deposits and withdrawals. If you have questions, ask! Just as you provide reviews and performance evaluations of your staff, do so for the financial team.

The worst thing you can do is just leave it all to the accountant and bookkeeper. Be proactive and get involved. Have things explained to you. It's not that hard. Just break through the fear and take it step by step. You made the decision to be the boss. You have the confidence and desire. You don't have to become an accountant or bookkeeper. Just be open to learning some basic principles and figure it out.

Client Expenses

This area applies mainly to personal injury and other contingency-based practices, but it's worth mentioning. In my firm, we front all the expenses for a case. My firm pays all costs, including court fees, medical record retrieval expenses, expert fees, deposition costs, trial costs, etc., during the life of a case. These costs can vary from $100 per case to $100,000, depending on the type, length and complexity of the case (which is also why we're extremely selective with the medical malpractice cases we sign up; they can run over $100,000 in expenses!). This expense item can become very large. Right now, I have about $2,000,000 in client expenses floating out there. Those are my after-tax dollars being used to fund existing cases. So, what does that number mean to my business?

Simply put, it's a loan I'm giving to all my clients to prosecute their cases. My retainer gives them a choice to either pay their own case expenses or have my firm foot that bill. In my career, I have yet to retain a client who chose to personally pay expenses. So, each payment I make on their cases is really loan, since I am getting that money back when we resolve the case. It comes out of the settlement or award. If we lose, they don't pay me back.

I'll throw this out there as well: You can earn money on this. Since these expenses really are loans, you can charge your client interest on these amounts, but you must spell that out in your retainer. It's perfectly fine to charge reasonable interest on this money. After all, a case can take years to resolve. By paying all the expenses, you're essentially providing an interest-free loan to the client for the duration of the case.

As a business proposition, that's a winning deal for the client and a losing deal for you. Money has a time value to it. That's why banks and insurance companies are the richest industries in the world. They play with interest rates and time values every day. There's nothing wrong with charging interest for a loan. In the business world, you'd be stupid not to.

All that said, I don't charge my clients interest on these expenses. I've seriously considered it and do have it spelled out in my retainer. But I have yet to enforce it. As a businessman, I want to, but as a lawyer representing injury victims, I haven't been able to pull the trigger on that one. At this point, it just doesn't feel good to me. That's my only explanation. It certainly doesn't make business sense, but it's the consensus of how my partners and I feel about the issue (I can already hear Connie sharpening her pencil!).

Credit Cards And Lines Of Credit

Speaking of loans, let's talk about the loans you may need to start or grow your business. The most common sources are credit cards and lines of credit. Credit cards are useful because you can delay the payment of expenses, but the bill for the card comes due every month. If you don't pay the full bill, the balance is carried over, with interest. On the other hand, a line of credit is issued by a bank and allows you to draw down money you need, but again, you pay monthly interest on the outstanding balance. Which is better?

Here's what you need to know about these choices: CREDIT CARD INTEREST RATES ARE ASTRONOMICAL! Bank rates for lines of credit are usually a fraction of credit card rates. It's a no-brainer, people! Don't carry balances on the credit cards. Use the line of credit.

I learned this the hard way. When I took over the business operations of my firm, I saw that our credit cards were maxed out, but we did have room on our line of credit. Why? Who knows? A quick analysis of the situation revealed that the balances carried on the credit cards were being charged over 16% interest per month, but the line of credit interest rate was just over 4%! Why were we paying 4x the interest on our money when we had this choice? I don't know! On that day, I instructed the bookkeeper to NEVER carry a balance on ANY credit card, so long as we had room on the line of credit. Ever since that day, we've never carried a balance on a credit card.

Of course, if you're starting a new business and a bank refuses to issue a line of credit or gives you a limited one, you may not have this choice. But keep an eye on all the credit card balances and pay as much as you can. Every few months, check with your bank regarding that line of credit (getting it or upping it). Soon enough, as the business grows, you'll be able to establish the line that you need.

My advice: Embrace the business side of law. Get over the fear of numbers. It's your money. Nobody cares about it as much as you.

CREATE YOUR OWN IDEAL INCOME

This is your business. Not the bookkeeper's or the accountant's, but *your* business. Remember that. Why? As Jeff mentioned, lawyers don't pay enough attention to their own finances. It makes you wonder how are they running their businesses? That's why we're writing this book! The message is clear: don't be ignorant of your numbers and don't rely on anyone to know your business better than you. They won't and they can't.

Become aware of all the internal workings of everything. I'm not saying it's your responsibility to micro-manage, but what I am saying is, educate yourself on everything. Know and understand how you make money and where you spend it. You don't have to know exactly what everyone is doing every minute of every day. Just be aware and stay involved. No one is more invested in your business and success than you are. Ever. Remember that.

The money you make is the lifeline of the business. Without a profit, you have no business. To run a business effectively and efficiently you need a plan. What's your plan?

Numbers, Numbers, Numbers

Jeff and I always laugh about business numbers. Not because it's funny, but because I have a different approach on the subject. Jeff is super-analytical and very realistic. I, on the other hand, I am not. I say this in a good way, since it's the key to the growth of our partnership, both personally and professionally. He encourages me in ways I could not, and I encourage him in ways he could not. Our relationship is a blending of maximizing both our views, and it works for us.

My view on the financials is a bit more simplified compared to Jeff's version. Jeff breaks it down to Profit/Loss and Balance Sheet business stuff. This is certainly important for any business. BUT so often, businesses neglect to do the FIRST thing that really matters: Create the proper mindset for the level of success you want to achieve, as opposed to the level of success you "think" you can attain.

Visualize Your Ideal Money Goal

Everything starts with a vision. Everything. The problem is that most people don't invest the time in creating a vision. So, they end up with a business by default. There's a huge difference between *creating* a business and *reacting* to the business. Creating is much more fun, easy, and definitive. Reacting is inconsistent, exhausting, and gets you as far as a hamster on a running wheel. Which do you prefer?

"Creating" a business proves more successful in the long run. Why on earth would anyone choose to react rather than create? You'd be surprised. Most people don't know how to create or to visualize. Most people are unaware how powerful personal intentions really are in life and in business. But you, my friends, are hearing it here first: This is the best way to effectively start your business. You can do this at any time in your business. And you can do this now, even if you haven't started your own business yet!

What the heck am I talking about? Let me ask you: How much money do you "want" to make next year? Not how much you "think" you will make. That's an important distinction because so often people use their current or past reality as a benchmark for what they believe they can achieve in the future. Your past earnings are not an accurate benchmark. That kind of thought actually holds you back from making more money. Why? Because your mind is limiting your potential to earn more by using false parameters of what is attainable by you, based on your limited thinking.

In general, when we hold a job and receive a salary, we create a belief that our source of income comes from that alone. So, if our annual salary is $85,000, in our minds that's what we're going to make in a year. No more, no less. By doing this, we are closing off other ways of receiving money. But money can come to us in different forms.

If you limit how you think about money and you believe, "I must work hard and struggle in order to make money," guess what happens? You won't make money unless you work hard and struggle. BUT, if you believe in the power of your mind and your intention of the vision you want for your life, then and only then will you allow money to flow to you in all forms. You simply need to be open to receiving it in any way possible.

How to do this? It's easy, but it will require expanding your mindset a bit!

What's your ideal yearly income? Fill it in the space below, but before you do, remember, the number must be more than you currently earn and should excite you. However, at this point, the number shouldn't be outlandish, because then you'll never believe it. For now, make it believable to you. Otherwise, you'll feel defeated before you even begin. That defeats the whole purpose of this.

$_____ (fill it in or say it out loud)

I will assume you came up with a number that stretched your imagination a bit but doesn't feel impossible. Great!

Actions To Make Your Vision Your Reality

Now, in order to create that income, what are some actionable steps you can take towards achieving your desired income level? These actionable steps do NOT have to produce income, but they must be ways in which you are going to elevate your brand: YOU.

The goal is to put your energy into building YOU, the brand, which in turn will reflect in your income opportunities. Maybe not right now, but definitely later. Also, the more attention you give to elevating YOU, the more you open yourself up to new opportunities and income potential.

Here are some simple and easy ways you can start contributing to your income goal. Again, it's not about the actual income producing you do, it is more about the "energy" you invest in going outside your comfort zone or what's considered as your "norm." The more focused, clear energy you invest towards growing your brand (aka your income level), the more opportunities you will attract.

To simplify, you get back what you put out. Both positive and negative. So, if you *worry* about making money and being successful, you squash any chance of opportunity. Conversely …

Put Positive, Excited Energy Towards Making Money And Being Successful In Order To Attract Positive, Money-Making Opportunities.

Examples:

Write and submit articles to local publications. Position yourself as the expert. This literally is the EASIEST thing to do. Why people don't take more advantage of this, I'll sadly never understand. PS: It's also free. Free. And free. ALWAYS take advantage of FREE advertising.

Reach out to CLE (continuing legal education) companies and offer to give free lectures. You might be thinking it's a waste of time if you're not getting anything out of it but, it's a great opportunity to meet other lawyers and get business referred to you in the future. Again, you are positioning yourself as an expert (not just an ABOGADO).

Post on social media. It's free advertising and it reminds people what you do. Be your own press. Build your own brand. Remember, it's okay to mix personal and business. People prefer working with people they know and trust. Let people into your life. People enjoy seeing your happy, fun life or happy family moments.

Some DON'TS of social media: Don't be a jerk EVER. It's called being a human. Don't post things that are political or mean to anyone or anything. You are building your brand. Happy, upbeat is what people are most attracted to. You are creating that life so stick with that as your benchmark. If you're unsure, DON'T POST IT. And if you disagree with a post, DON'T COMMENT. You don't want to come across as that crazy social media person. That's negative energy and you don't want to radiate it.

Submit to some of these nonsensical "award" opportunities (like Top Lawyer, Super-Great Attorneys, Top Leader awards). Some people are easily impressed with these things. I find this strange, since many of these awards are pay-to-play (which most people don't realize), but it does add to you being recognized. Who doesn't want that? As your brand and business grows, you probably won't participate in as many pay-to-play awards and events, but if you are getting started, they are great opportunities for good press and networking.

Participate in your law school's alumni program. It's a great way to connect with other alumni and attend fun events.

Join your local chamber of commerce. Join the board. Position yourself as the town's lawyer. Get involved in your neighborhood. Become the neighborhood lawyer everyone knows and trusts.

When it comes to groups and organizations, try them out. Join and become active in Bar Associations, Charitable Organizations, and non-profits. You won't see a benefit overnight but stick with it. See what comes from it. Just like anything, you may and will outgrow these. When you see that your participation is no longer the best use of your time, resign.

Embrace your heritage. Join groups associated with your heritage and gain support. Become a leader within that community.

Create a personal website that features your accomplishments and involvements. Again, just a reminder, don't measure your success on this stuff. Instead, use it as an encouragement to highlight yourself in a way that helps promote you and your business. Writing a blog on your website pertaining to your practice area helps increase SEO (search engine optimization) and being found in a Google search. Another WIN-WIN.

Join your favorite sports club (like tennis, golf, etc.). Make sure people know what you do for a living. Connect. Make new friends and network while learning or playing a sport you enjoy.

Create a podcast. Again, this positions you as the expert. Develop weekly shows specific to your area of law. Invite different guests to educate on other areas of the law. This develops you as a leader in your industry.

And anything else you could think of. Seriously, the sky is the limit here.

Try things out and see what works. Some will, some won't. And some will just work for a period of time. That's okay and that's life. Only you know what's best for you. And as you grow, what's best for you will evolve. Go with the flow but be open to trying things out. You just never know.

Move outside your comfort zone. When you go beyond your everyday "norm," you're inviting new experiences into your life. Be proud of yourself when you do this, even if it's as small as getting a coffee from Starbucks as opposed to Dunkin. Take a different route to work. Reach out to old contacts. Sounds silly, I know, but it works. When you break your normal routine and go outside your comfort zone, you shift your energy and allow for new opportunity.

These are some possible options of how you can elevate your brand. Investing in this kind of energy leads to your ideal income goal. What are some things you can start today? Take the time now, while this material is fresh in your mind, and list five things you will do for the upcoming year to elevate your brand and achieve your income goal:

1. _____

2. _____

3. _____

4. _____

5. _____

JEFF CHAPTER FIVE

DO YOU NEED A PARTNER?

In law school, my only professional goal was to "make partner" at a big firm. I never really thought past that. The only thing I associated with "making partner" was money. First year associates at the big firms earned huge salaries, which increased every year. In my mind, the harder I worked, the more likely I'd "make partner" in about seven years, the traditional route. Networking and relationship building were completely foreign concepts.

Looking back at my big summer job after the second year of law school, I was utterly clueless about that firm! I never noticed how many people were employed there. I generally knew of the number of attorneys and different departments but had no idea how much income the firm earned. I couldn't tell you anything about the staff or how the firm was set up or managed. Expenses? Who cared? I wasn't even balancing my own checkbook at that time (remember, I hadn't yet held a full-time job in my life!). All I knew was to keep my head down, stay focused on whatever project was in front of me, and work work work work work! I was living the life of a professional student.

Alas, I didn't get the full-time job offer at summer's end, which was the best thing that ever happened. Thankfully, I engaged in some self-reflection and considered, "what do I like to do?" and "what am I good at?" My answer: Trials! I was always a good public speaker and loved competition! Fortunately, I landed a job at the Bronx County District Attorney's Office, where I learned about trying cases (and a lot more about building relationships). My "business" education came later.

What's Your Path?

So, what's your path? If you're a student, what do you want to do? What do you like? What do you enjoy? What makes you happy? What are you good at? Are you utilizing your natural skills? If you're an associate somewhere, same questions: Happy? Love it? Look forward to going to work? Is your ideal future where you are now? Do you want something different? Do you want to be the boss?

Let me be clear here: Not everyone wants to or should be the boss. Starting a firm, growing a firm, managing a firm, being a boss – that's not a job everyone wants or should want. Many people shudder at the idea of that kind of responsibility. Having a secure job and enjoying the work is all that many people need to be truly happy and satisfied. Guess what? THAT'S GREAT! I mean it. And if that's you, guess what else? YOU'RE NOT ALONE. Statistically and factually, there are tons more workers than bosses. It's not even close.

But if you're reading this book, you are at least harboring thoughts of being the boss. You're entertaining the thought of going solo and running a business. Can you do it alone? You're on the path to potential partnership and want to know more about what that means.

Start Small

Let's start with the small firm stuff. Do you want to go it alone, or do you want to find a business partner? It's a big decision. There's something to be said for creating a lean, mean office from the ground up as a solo practitioner. There's less staff, less overhead, less headaches. You keep pretty much what you kill. If that's attractive to you, then go for it.

What kind of person are you? Do you like to work alone? Are you comfortable making every decision? Does it pain you to think about writing a check to an employee or two each week? If so, then solo practice probably works. I know plenty of solos comfortable making all the decisions. Some set up shop with zero full time employees. All staff are either part-timers, per diem or outside consultants. That's lean: no commitment, no benefits, no strings attached. Many solos share office space and share reception and administrative personnel. With technology advances (and a recent pandemic), it's possible (and easy) to go without an office. I know a person outsourcing medical records requests to a company in Bosnia! Not sure of the cost for that, but it's less than the minimum wage here.

The biggest challenge in starting a firm from the ground up is MONEY. How do you pay for anything before the business is up and running? You haven't started yet! Without a family member or a bank loaning you startup money, it's tough.

Many solos start out working for a solo (or small firm), knowing the goal is to leave when the time is right. For law school graduates, that gives you time to learn a field, make money, save money, establish relationships, and plan your future. You confirm that the field you're in is the field for you. Or not. It's a good way to eliminate an area of practice you don't like.

Perhaps most importantly, this path gives you an opportunity to learn a business. If your goal is to be the boss, watch and learn what the boss is doing. Ask questions. Take notice. Be observant. Listen to what is said. How does the firm make money? How did the firm get all these matters or cases? What's going on to get new business?

A new case doesn't just magically appear. Somebody was responsible for bringing that case in. Who? How? What's the connection? What's the origin of that connection? How was that connection cultivated? Why does that connection continue to refer cases? What's the incentive for anyone to refer a case to the firm?

Be Careful

Time for a word of caution. Some of these questions cannot be asked out loud. Understandably, the boss may be reluctant to give up all this information. A boss may feel threatened by some of these questions. Sources of business are extremely valuable. People work very hard establishing relationships that lead to business. Be sensitive to that.

Here's my story on this subject: My first job after the District Attorney's Office was with an insurance defense firm. Almost all its clients were insurance companies or municipal entities (I wasn't consciously aware of that until after I left). I was the junior associate on "team" led by a senior partner, junior partner, and senior associate. My goal: to please everyone above me with hard work and billable hours.

I knew nothing about how the business came in. I made fast friends with many of the junior and senior associates. We ate lunch together and spoke often about the firm's politics. I heard about clients and "keeping them happy." To me, that meant writing good status reports and promptly returning their calls.

However, soon I learned that insurance company "X" recently reduced its referrals from 20 cases a month to 10 and that insurance company "Y" just tripled their referrals to us. And that we just entered into a new agreement with New York City to handle more municipal cases. It made me wonder, how does that happen? Who's responsible for that? How do these companies even know we exist?

At the office holiday party, I approached a name partner, someone I had never spoken with before. I introduced myself and started some small talk. And then, I simply asked the question, "How can I get an insurance company to give us business; how does that work?" His eyes widened. He looked perplexed. He took a step back and measured me up before finally responding, "You just do the work; I'll worry about bringing in the business."

That was my moment of clarity. My "aha" moment in business. Right then, I knew my time at that firm was done. I realized that the earnings ceiling there was very low. My opportunity for growth and more money was extremely limited. The business owners weren't interested in new partners. They just wanted more workers. And, hey, that's fine! Lots of people working there weren't remotely interested in being business owners. Most were content with their jobs and their outlooks. But for me, the light bulb went on.

Solo Pitfalls

Let's return to the solos. This is a big deal for you folks. Let's say you took that huge step and started your own business! You made connections, the work is coming in, and you're growing. So much so, you feel a bit overwhelmed. Your days fly by. You think, "it's 5:00 p.m. already! I just got here." It feels like there aren't enough hours in a day. You wake up earlier, stop taking vacations, and find yourself recharging your cell phone battery in the middle of the day.

You can become a victim of your own success. Every new case or matter you sign up takes away time to spend on the existing ones. At some point, you must delegate. Well, first you need people around you. Have you hired anyone yet?

Let's assume you rent space, share administrative help with other solos and small firms in the suite and hired a part-time paralegal. For court appearances, depositions, and some other tasks, you hire per diem workers to cover you. Great job keeping the costs down. Nevertheless, you can't be everywhere, and you can't do everything.

So, you hire your first attorney. To save money, it's a fresh, new law school graduate. She's eager, ready, willing, and able. When she shows up, you immediately realize she knows nothing about your business! In fact, she knows nothing about business in general! In law school, she participated in moot court and clerked part time for a federal magistrate. What does either have to do with your business? Probably nothing! So, what does that mean?

You must *train* her. You hired her because you didn't have time to work on your cases, but now must take the time to train her. How long does that take? Why does it feel like you're going backwards? Were you better off going it alone and just becoming more selective in the cases signed on? Maybe.

Maintaining a lean caseload with high value cases works. But as a solo, it's all about relationships. Maybe rejecting cases isn't good for business. Your mindset is to please everyone, because you never know who's going to need your services next. You feel that if you reject someone's case, they'll never come back to you again. You want to grow, but you want to save money, but you need the help, but you have to train the help, so maybe you don't need to hire, but you're getting business, but it may be too much business, so you don't turn down anything, and your caseload keeps growing, and you're back to needing help. HELLLLPPPP!!!

What's the answer? Well, what's a lawyer's answer to every question? It depends. If you reach this point as a solo, you need some self-reflecting. What do you want? What makes you happy? And be honest! Don't answer what you think is right, or what your spouse thinks is right or what your mother would want. Keep those voices out of your head!

The only voice that matters is yours. Think about what's best for you! Are you most happy in business as a solo or small practice? Do you like the "compact" nature of that kind of practice? Is growing and delegating something that doesn't interest you? That's cool. But you still must do something if you've reached that "Help" point.

Let's say you've tried growing and it just hasn't worked. Let's assume it doesn't feel good and it's not what makes you happy. Given my example above, you'd have to scale back the cases you sign up. You'd have to be more selective about the cases you take. Becoming a boutique type firm, with a narrow focus in a specific area, can be terrific and wildly successful. But you'd have to start turning cases down. You'd have to get over the "but I want everyone to like me" feeling. In this type of business, you need everyone to *respect* you and your special skills. More importantly, YOU must respect you and your special skills. You must believe in that wholeheartedly. It really works.

Be Selective

In my firm, as we've grown, I've become more selective with the medical malpractice cases we've taken on. Those cases are extremely costly and time consuming. Losing a medical malpractice case after verdict can cost over $100,000, which I'm not getting back. Losing a couple of those a year can really hurt the bottom line. So, we've raised the threshold of what constitutes a case for us.

Guess what? I haven't lost any referring attorneys. I learned to say "no," they learned to hear "no," and they respect me for it. Now they're more excited when I actually take a case! What are they doing with the cases I reject? I'm not sure. If they find another attorney to take the case, good for them! A pessimist would worry: What if that other attorney gets a great result? Would the referring attorney now send all the business to that person? Maybe. But I'm not thinking that way. I know what's good for me. I know what's good for my business. I have CONFIDENCE in the parameters I've set for my business.

That kind of confidence is contagious within your business. That kind of confidence affects how people perceive you. More importantly, it makes you feel good. So, my thought process? If I reject a case that someone else takes, great. If that attorney achieves a huge award for the client, terrific. I still know I made the right decision for me and my firm. There must have been some reason why I rejected the case, or another attorney took the case – maybe that client wouldn't have been a good fit for us on an emotional level; maybe some other lawyer was a better fit, maybe this, maybe that. At the end of the day, it doesn't matter to me. I did what was best for my firm in that moment. I own that decision and I'm moving on.

So, you determined solos and small practitioners, keep going! But be confident and wear that confidence proudly! You can do it!

Partnership Benefits

I love the benefits of having a partner. It's a way to collaborate, co-create and brainstorm. Building something as a team is incredibly rewarding. It's fun to share success!

Partnerships work beautifully when each partner brings a different skill set to the table. For law firms (and really any business), multiple skill sets create a successful organization. For one, the firm must have good lawyers; people who know the law and possess the skills relevant to the practice. You must be good in field you chose! Law firms provide a service to their clients. All the skills necessary to provide that service in a competent, compassionate, diligent manner are important.

But then, there's the business aspect of the firm. Aside from whatever law makes up the practice of the firm, it's a business that needs to be run. Don't ever underestimate that! Somebody must oversee and manage the business. Someone must make sure the income is exceeding the expenses!

My point? Your firm is more likely to achieve this kind diversity of talent with more than one person at the helm. The best firms have partners who can spread their talents, focus on their assets and attributes, and collectively create a well-oiled machine.

In my field, for example, people differentiate between the "inside" lawyers and the "outside" lawyers. The "inside" lawyer is running the business end of things. Think: Managing Partner. That's who spends more time in the office working ON the business instead of IN the business. Someone working ON the business reviews the profit/loss sheet with the accountant, ensures the cash flow is meeting the firm's needs and maximizes the efficiencies of the firm. The "outside" lawyers are the ones who go to court every day, make appearances at conferences, do depositions, and try cases. They're IN the business of personal injury law, doing what most personal injury lawyers do on a daily basis.

Regardless of where you fall between these categories, the need for networking and rainmaking skills applies to everyone. Whether you're "inside" or "outside," bringing in business is important.

As an "outside" person, you may naturally interact with more people outside the firm. Being in court and attending depositions naturally puts you with a lot of people who can send business to the firm. Every encounter outside the firm is an opportunity to showcase your skills, personality and connect with someone.

The "inside" people establish their networks through bar association events, lecturing, other speaking engagements, bar association committee work, volunteer or non-profit work and a host of other opportunities. Be creative! And don't underestimate golf. I've seen the wonders of establishing a rapport and relationship on the golf course. It's a real thing, people! Go work on your swing!

Like any relationship, the partnership needs nurturing. Like any relationship, communication is key. Like any relationship, you need to have each other's backs. I truly like and trust my partners. Maybe you didn't choose your partners. Say, for example, you join a firm as an associate and rise through the ranks to partner. You may not "click" with all the existing partners. That's ok. Be open to new relationships. Treat your partners as you want to be treated. Stay positive and put the partnership's interests first.

Transition To Partner

I experienced a "social" transition when I became a partner. One day I was an associate, interacting mostly with the other associates and staff. We all got along and socialized after work. What did we talk about? The bosses, of course! How this one did that, the other one didn't do something else. You know the drill! But then, one day I became a boss. Management! I was one of them.

It literally happens overnight. The decision comes and you arrive the next day as a partner. That does and should change the way you view the workplace. Not that you suddenly shun your former associates and treat your staff differently. But now, your allegiance and loyalties are changed. Your partners need to know you are on *their* side. They need to know that you look out for them. They need to know that you look out for the best interests of the firm. You need to know that your interests equal those of the firm.

Partnership Agreements

To become a partner, do you need a formal written agreement (contract)? No, but should you have one? What do YOU think? You're a lawyer! Of course, you need a contract! You'd be shocked to learn how many small partnerships don't have contracts. I get it: It's not something you want to think about. Like a prenuptial agreement, it's not a great topic to cover. Also, you may need to enlist (and pay) another lawyer. Heaven, forbid! But guess what? It's money well spent. Do it.

I joined an existing 2-person partnership that had no contract. Two guys, same age, same generation, same relative background, same goals, similar financial needs … you get the picture. They were like brothers. And everything was 50/50. Pretty easy stuff.

Then I came along. After years of proving my worth, they invited me to join the partnership. I was much younger than they were, different generation, different background, different financial situation, different goals … you get the picture again. And I was a third wheel. An uneven number! How to make decisions now? Vote on everything? Should we use secret ballots?

I didn't care. I was excited and proud as ever – a partner in my own business! I achieved a huge goal of mine! I loved these guys. It was always like working with my dad and uncle. Now they were my partners. I just wanted to hug them and start working! Instead, we all lawyered up!

Huh? It felt weird. Our first official act as partners? Hiring lawyers to figure out how to end the partnership should one of us die, retire, or become disabled. Whoo hoo!!

Several meetings with our lawyers in a strange conference room took months. We sat on opposite sides of the table! Their lawyer drafted an agreement, which I reviewed with my lawyer. I negotiated against the guys I loved; the guys that helped me fulfill a lifelong dream. Was this the beginning of a beautiful relationship? It didn't feel like Casablanca. ☺

As surreal as it seemed, the process was necessary. We all felt better after the agreement was signed and we haven't looked at it since. But we all know it's there if an issue arises.

Issues To Address In The Partnership Agreement

What are the issues to address in a partnership agreement? The biggest three are death, disability, and retirement. What happens with each event? Back to the answer that lawyers love: It depends. Every partnership is different. That's why you need counsel to address your specific needs and concerns. It's a give and take, like every other negotiation.

For me, the initial concern was decision-making. Since I joined two guys who had been partners for 20 years and loved each other like brothers, I figured to lose every vote 2-1. They had a wonderful, successful partnership and were just fine without me. On any important decision, they would surely agree. I wouldn't have a say in anything.

How did we deal with that? Our agreement spelled out the decisions requiring a "super majority" or a unanimous vote. It was a short list, but an important one. It included decisions about bringing in another equity partner, certain money decisions, capital contributions and changing the firm name.

Here's the funny thing about all that. I soon learned that while my partners loved each other like brothers, they also fought like brothers. Not in a bad way. In a good way, actually. They took every decision seriously and hashed out all the issues between them. Behind closed doors, they disagreed on almost everything! Which cases to accept or reject, valuing cases, strategic and tactical calls, office protocol, ethical questions, budget issues and most importantly, what to have for lunch. They didn't agree on anything! The practical effect of all this? I made every decision! I would listen to each of their arguments and the one I agreed with, won. Suddenly, I was calling all the shots!

My advice: Create a partnership agreement. Even if you partner up with someone your age, in the same financial situation, family structure and future goals, do it. Take the time to consider the issues and put them on paper. It's good business.

VISUALIZE ALL YOUR GOALS

Jeff just walked you through a big decision: Should you seek a partner or go solo? I'm going to take a step back on that. This decision was important for Jeff because he established "partnership" as a goal. As he mentioned, he wasn't even sure what that meant, being a "partner." Nevertheless, he was clear on what he wanted. And importantly, his thoughts and understanding about that goal shifted as his career progressed.

That's what I focus on with my clients: Setting goals, being clear, visualizing, and staying open to wherever life takes you – those are keys to genuine happiness and success.

What Is Your Ideal Vision Of Your Life?

My goal in this chapter: Expand your thinking. That may sound airy-fairy, but only to those who never pursue their hopes and dreams. You are different. You are meant to thrive, be happy, and become uber-successful!

Every single person has this ability. Unfortunately, some people never learn the information you are reading here, aren't open to change, and just accept their unfulfilled life as is. They never realize they have an opportunity to make their lives better. It's as if they believe that having goals only sets them up for disappointment if those goals are not reached.

In fact, the opposite is true. Our vision of what we want drives us internally for more and for better. It's not that you're never satisfied. You are always satisfied, but ALSO always eager for more. That's the joy and fun of work AND life!

Are you ready? It's time for you to take some action toward creating your ideal life! Be open in thinking in a bigger way! Don't forget, we kick reality out the door for this exercise. This is all about what you WANT; not to be mistaken for what you "think" you can have. Don't be fearful or bashful in what you write down. Instead, challenge yourself to embrace your goals and allow your mind to contemplate the life you want. The life you truly deserve.

If you become stuck on some questions, no worries. Just use it as a gauge for something to think about. You can always come back to this exercise once you finish the book. And also, like in everything I teach, you are always allowed to change your mind. It's your life. Nothing is set in stone. Sometimes one goal morphs into something else as your confidence and belief grow within. The purpose of this exercise is to just get you started.

As you answer the questions below, there are some guidelines. *Do not use your current life or past life as benchmarks for your future potential.* Right then and there, you limit yourself, especially knowing that loving and appreciating *you* (not anyone else) is your top priority. Your ideal vision and potential are by-products of what you believe to be possible.

Forget your current job or your career path up to now. Forget your past relationships. Forget what you grew up with. Forget anyone or anything that could limit your potential. Take a moment and wipe all that from your mind.

Just take a second to open your mind to what would really make you happy in this life. Decide what kind of life you want for yourself. That's right! Just think about it and make a decision. You can have exactly what you want. Now answer these questions. Be specific.

Q. How do you want to feel every day when you wake up? List 5 adjectives to describe best how you want to feel when starting your day.

A. _____

_____

_____

Q. Who do you want to "be" showing up to your life every day? List 5 characteristics/qualities you either have or want to develop to be your happiest, truest self.

A. _____

_____

_____

Q. Work life: Do you want a solo law practice? Want to manage other lawyers? Want to build an empire? Want to be a TV personality? The next Judge Judy? Want to be an author? Professor? What do you really want? What will you *love* doing?

A._____

_____

_____

Q. Personal life: What does your ideal family life looks like? Are you alone or in a relationship? Is your work separate from your life partner's? Or is it intertwined with that person? Where do you live? What car do you drive? What do you really want? What will make you really happy?

A._____

_____

_____

BIG CONGRATS on completing your "Ideal Vision."

Make Your Vision A Reality!

It may take some time to adjust to this type of thinking. It's not how most people are conditioned to think. In the beginning of our relationship, Jeff often told me to "be realistic." He knows better now! Being "realistic" holds you back. Anything is possible if you just believe it is.

It's more than a thought process. Make it real for you. How? Is there a dream house in your mind? Go check out some homes on the market in that neighborhood. Even if the cost is 10 times what you can afford (for now), who cares? Go check it out. Nobody needs to know you can't afford it now. Go there. See it. Walk around. Ask questions. Visualize yourself living there. Connect with how that makes you feel. Harness that feeling. Remember it.

What's that one car you'd love to have? Go to the dealership. Sit in the driver's seat. Smell the interior. Take a test drive. Connect with how that makes you feel. Harness that feeling. Remember it.

Ever thought about a custom suit or outfit? The "bespoke" industry is very competitive. Save a little money and go for it. Have the rep come to your home (they most likely will). Go through the process: Have all the measurements taken, look through the fabric books, touch, and feel the different textures. Just buy one (even though the salesperson will push for 2 or 3). See what happens when that suit arrives. Put it on. Connect with how that makes you feel. Harness that feeling. Remember it.

Get rid of all the clothes that don't serve your goals and vision. Lose all the stuff that doesn't serve your new lifestyle and vision of where you want to go. A clear vision allows you to clean house and rid yourself of the extras. Clarity enables you to turn down opportunities that don't belong on the path to your goals.

Make your vision part of your narrative. Talk about it! Saying things out loud contributes to making them real. Talk about the job you want, the career you want, the car you want, the home you want, the life you want. Believe it. Be confident about it.

Work Smart, NOT Hard

Visualizing our hopes and dreams and putting them to paper creates the framework for our future success. Once the goal is clear, you make better decisions on the best use of your time. Clear goals allow you to focus on the actions necessary to make your dreams a reality. It's as simple as that. This is how life becomes easier for you. When you are crystal clear about your vision, you stop wasting time doing things that don't contribute to your ultimate goal.

That's the leverage of working smart, NOT hard. When you work smart, you use your mind to your advantage. You become super-focused on your vision and allow that purpose to lead the way. Life becomes more enjoyable because you work towards something meaningful to you. When you work hard without clear intentions, you spin your wheels and waste your energy. You become deflated, disappointed, and overworked, with no real results.

I already hear people thinking, "Success without hard work? That sounds like B.S." Yes, there are people who believe that. Of course, many people have achieved success through hard work. But there's an easier way to achieve success, so why not try it?

When you embrace my philosophy and feel good first, the actions you take are NOT hard. You become so excited about YOU and the possibilities of your life, that you are inspired to take the steps to move you forward. And in the process, you appreciate and enjoy the journey so you can be happy NOW and later.

Isn't that the point? *You want to be happy now, because when you are, life becomes easier.* Things tend to work out for you. Your attitude towards life changes. Instead of focusing on your challenges, you focus on your wins, little or big. Once you feel good, you realize everything is a win, even if it may not seem so in the moment. Every time something seems to be going wrong, it isn't. It's actually inspiring you and allowing you to change course to make it right.

Why The (So-Called) Problems That Arise Move You *TOWARDS* Your Vision

Consider these scenarios:

1. Your vision is to run your own firm or be your own boss. After 10 years at your current firm, you are fired. How do you feel? What do you think?

Either:

A)   You feel like a failure, resent your current employer, or remain in disbelief that you were fired after so many loyal years. "Where did I go wrong?" "I'll never get another job." **(negative mindset)**

Or

B)   "HOLY CRAP! Maybe this is the sign I needed that I am ready! Perhaps I outgrew my current firm. Maybe I no longer matched up with what they were looking for. It only makes sense that I would leave at some point. Plus, deep down inside I know if they did not fire me, I never would have made the jump to quit and be my own boss. I'm going to take advantage of this opportunity!" **(Start Loving Life® mindset)**

2. Your vision is to work in a fun environment where you are appreciated and valued. Instead, you work for jerk bosses who don't appreciate you and the company's morale stinks. Every day your boss is on your case and the firm's business is taking a nose-dive. How do you feel? What do you think?

Either:

A)   You feel like crap every day after being yelled at. You complain and whine to anyone who listens. You chalk up every unhappy client to poor leadership. You collect your paycheck and go home miserably every day. **(negative mindset)**

Or

B) Appreciate that running a business is not easy. Understand that the bosses are under a lot of pressure. Become clear that this firm is not the ideal work culture for your vision. Despite the conditions, continue to do your best at work. Spend your evenings updating your resume and looking for open positions at more ideal companies on LinkedIn. Secretly know that if work conditions weren't so bad, you probably would settle at this current firm a lot longer than you should. Remain focused at work, but even more focused on finding a better and more suitable job elsewhere **(Start Loving Life® mindset)**

3. Your vision is to be a well-respected top trial attorney. The main partner in your firm second-guesses your decisions on cases. Lately, you have become an easy target. How do you feel? What do you think?

Either:

A) You feel diminished, embarrassed, and like an idiot. You're more insecure than ever. You are afraid to speak up or make any decisions. You think you will never be a good trial attorney. You feel hopeless. **(negative mindset)**

Or

B) Try your best NOT to feel bad or take it personally. Instead, be open to learning from what's happening. Take this as a sign to learn your cases better. Make a point of asking the partner some well thought-out questions such as, how to handle specific cases to improve your thought process for future cases. Understand that to be a trial lawyer you must get used to rejection and questioning. Utilize this experience as a guide on how to better develop yourself in an uncomfortable situation. See that this situation is actually preparing you to be one AMAZING, TOUGH Trial Lawyer!

Devote the time to develop your interpersonal skills and confidence. Realize that one day you will look back at this partner and appreciate the positive impact this scenario had on your successful trial career. (**Start Loving Life® mindset**)

Instead of looking at things happening to you as negative, do your best to see the real reason things are happening FOR you. It keeps pushing you towards your ideal vision. If you are caught up in thinking that things are negative, you will never receive the true gift being given.

Begin to look at things differently. Start thinking positively. What does that even mean? Find the benefit in everything that happens in your life. You can, once you start feeling good about you. It just requires a strong sense of self and confidence within. Focus on the first and only thing that matters to ensure that your goals and visions become a reality: YOU.

College Hoops – Great Example

What do I know about college basketball? Nothing. What does Jeff know about it? A lot. What does the 1983 N.C. State NCAA championship season have to do with all this? Everything.

Jeff told me the story of this team and its journey that year. It's so amazing! They were a mediocre team all year but finished strong and made it to the NCAA Basketball Tournament. March Madness! They were huge underdogs but advanced to the finals where they played the Houston Cougars, the top ranked team in the nation. In an incredible upset, N.C. State won.

What's the big deal? N.C. State's coach, Jim Valvano, motivated them to believe in themselves. Despite the overwhelming odds against them, he convinced them they were destined to be champions. How? He just kept telling them that. But more importantly, he did something to connect them with the feeling of winning. He had them harness that feeling and remember it. How did he do that?

A long-standing college basketball tradition has the winning team cut down the nets from the baskets after the game. A ladder is rolled onto the court each team member snips some of the net from the basket. The last player puts the victorious net around his neck.

What did Jim Valvano do? After every practice during the tournament, he had the team practice cutting down the nets. They actually rolled out a ladder and each player participated in cutting the nets down. At first, the players thought it was nuts. They felt silly. But Valvano insisted they do it after every practice. Soon enough, something clicked. It began to feel good. They liked it. They even started to perform mock victory celebrations after the cutting. They hugged each other and danced around as if they had won.

What did Valvano's genius exercise do? It allowed them to visualize and feel what it would be like to win the national championship! They didn't just dream about it. They didn't just talk about it. They acted it out. It gave them a clear vision. It gave them confidence. They really believed they could win. And they did!

In life, you can have anything you want. There are so many opportunities for lawyers. Every business or industry has some connection to some area of law. People respect lawyers. Despite the stupid jokes out there, everyone needs and relies on a lawyer at some point in their lives. You have an expertise that people need. Your potential to succeed is limitless.

Now, will everyone be open to this way of thinking? Hell no! Most people (lawyers included) can't get out of their own way. If you repeat any of this information to anyone who is not open, they will think you are nuts. That's okay. This book isn't for them. This book was created specifically for lawyers like you who want more and know they deserve more; they just haven't figured out how ... until now!

Be A Partner Before Becoming One

THINK like a partner BEFORE you are one. If you do, the transition will be easier.

Be a true leader. That means be a leader before elevating to a leadership role. When you do, you improve your chances of that promotion!

Don't ever think like an employee. Ever. You wouldn't be reading this book if you were destined to be an employee forever. What does that mean? It means your attitude should never be "It's not my job" or "Why do I have to do this?"

*Here's a list of what you **shouldn't** do as an employee:*

- Complain
- Commiserate with others during the workday in the office
- Discuss your (or anyone else's) salary with anyone other than your boss
- Put your nose where it doesn't belong
- Contribute to drama
- Be negative
- Be problem-oriented instead of solution-oriented
- Say no to any extra work
- Watch the clock
- Leave exactly at 5:00 every night

Here's another one I love: Don't undermine your boss's decisions or company's policies OUT LOUD or to others. Some employees love to think they can run the company better and make better decisions. But instead of *doing* anything toward making that a reality someday, they just sit back, complain, collect their paycheck, and do nothing.

What these employees don't realize is that there are many different workings behind the scenes to which they are not privy. Guess what? LOTS of seemingly dumb decisions are actually made for reasons you may never understand or even want to know. You may never know why decisions or company policies are made until you are the boss. Until then, it's none of your business! But it is your business to support the company that cuts your check … and I'll explain why.

Always Be A Brand Ambassador

As an employee, by receiving a paycheck, you accept the role as an ambassador of your company. Your company is paying you to represent them on both personal and professional levels and in a positive manner. If for any reason you can't do that, then you shouldn't work there.

I'm not saying you will agree or should agree with everything your company does. I am sure you definitely won't. That's cool. Just don't go around speaking negatively about the company you work for. Ever. It's a reflection of them and YOU. If you don't love the company you work for, don't work for them. And if that's truly the case, silence is still the key.

Don't go around blabbing how you hate your company and crowing that you're looking for a new job. You come off negative and sound like a whiner. Even if you're right to feel that way, keep it to yourself. Use that feeling as motivation to find a new job, not to complain about the one you have.

When looking for a job, always speak highly of your current company. Your reasoning for leaving should always be the standard, "I enjoy/love my current role but there isn't opportunity for growth at this time," or something similar. Use your drive to succeed and past successes or achievements in your current role to sell a potential new employer. Don't ever focus or mention the REAL negative reasons why you want to leave, since the interviewer will just quickly assume that you'll say the same thing about them one day. Don't be that person.

More Of What You *SHOULD* Do

Do your job and more. Take initiatives! Learn as much as humanly possible about each position you hold and the workings of the firm. The more you know, the more valuable you are. The more valuable you are, the more leverage you have. Always.

Ask questions. People are often afraid to ask questions, fearing they will look "not smart." That itself is "not smart!" Show your interest and learn. Your boss will appreciate your desire to learn. If they don't, your boss isn't a good one. And you get to learn that as well.

Be mindful about *when* you ask questions. Certainly, don't start asking questions while your boss is in the middle of an unrelated crisis. If necessary, make a list of your questions and schedule an appointment to touch base with your boss to discuss. Your boss will eagerly comply. Or they may ask you to email them the questions to review. Either way, learn your boss's style on how to they prefer communication. It shows that you care and that you're proactive and respectful of their time. They will appreciate that and you.

Mind your own business. *Don't gossip.* Ever. It's none of your business. Don't make it your business. And it's karma. We all screw up. Would you want someone talking about you? Just don't talk about anyone in a negative way. Even if it's true. Your attitude is everything. Trying to maintain a positive one is always the key.

Don't be "judge-y" of anyone or anything. You never know what's going on behind the scenes or what someone is dealing with. Don't make assumptions. Instead, be supportive of others, regardless. Be the person who is always consistent in their demeanor, positive and professional.

If you stick with all this, your transition to partnership will be easy AND no surprise to anyone – because what I listed above, no one ever really does.

By taking this advice, you will separate yourself from the herd and people will view you as a leader. They may not say it to you, but it's true.

To transition to partner, attitude is everything. Play the role even before it's assigned and you'll be a shoo-in!

JEFF CHAPTER SIX

STAFFING NEEDS

Whether you're a solo or in a partnership, you're gonna need help! That means you gotta spend money! That's tough for a lot of people. Accept it. Get used to it. Just be smart about it.

Time for some more self-analysis. Ask yourself the following:

What am I good at in this business?

With what do I need help?

How can I make my firm more efficient?

How can I be more efficient?

Now think about last week and list all the tasks you performed each day. I'm not kidding, do it! All the tasks! Let's review the list. Which of those tasks:

Helped bring in business?

Directly brought in money?

Indirectly brought in money?

Moved cases closer to resolution?

Could have been performed only by you?

Could have been performed by another lawyer?

Could have been completed by a non-lawyer?

A few more – Which of those tasks:

Did you enjoy doing?

Made you happy?

Came naturally and required little effort?

Challenged you in a way you enjoy being challenged?

Felt menial?

Did you dread doing?

Would you be happy never doing again?

In any practice, as the firm grows, so do the mundane responsibilities: organizing case files, setting up new cases, filing documents with the court, copying and scanning, drafting and mailing correspondence, scheduling appointments, confirming appearances and appointments, etc. If you do these things yourself, they take over your entire day.

As a solo, the big jump is that first hire. When do you do it? In a growing firm, the question is when to create a new position (or add another staffer to share the workload). These are tough calls to make. But are they really? If you're in tune with yourself and your business, it should be obvious. Just take the time and think about it. Talk it out with a colleague or your partner. Think about what you want your days to be like; what you want to be doing; what will make you want to go to the office. If that's not happening, make that change!

Some people need physical evidence to provide the impetus to change. Go look at the finances! Check out the bottom line. Are you making money? Are you making more money than last year? Here's a good one: Look at the firm's net income over the last 3 years. Has it increased every year?

If your business is growing but your income is decreasing, there's your evidence! That could mean you're doing a great job getting new business, but you're not maximizing the value of the cases brought in. Why? You might not have the time or the help? You might be too busy running around, meeting with clients, signing up cases, going to court, doing paperwork, and returning phone calls to nurture the existing business. Thus, you certainly don't have time to be on top of the expenses and minimize those. A growing business losing money is a telltale sign of inefficiency. You need help!

When you're ready to hire, put together an organizational chart. Even if it's just you and one employee, set this up. Write out a job description to provide clarity to you and the employee. It makes clear your expectations from that position. It provides a broad perspective of the firm and how the wheels turn to make the machine go! It's a benchmark for expectations to use for year-end reviews and evaluations. At its core, it's another form of communication important for success.

With growth comes more work, more money, and more responsibility. As your company grows, place people in positions of authority: managers, supervisors, directors, etc. Reward the right people with money, titles, and responsibilities.

Delegating may be the toughest thing for an attorney to do – another one that's not taught in any law school. But it's imperative for a successful business owner to understand. It is what will keep you sane, healthy, and happy.

Part Timers

Start delegating by hiring part-time attorneys and paralegals to cover some work areas. Law student interns are a bright bunch of people, hungry, and looking for experience. We've hired many, several of whom later joined the firm as associates. While it does take some time to train them, they're generally good fits. One thing we always do, though, is PAY THEM!

Law schools are finally beginning to offer more internship and externship programs, giving students some real-life experience. Many now obtain credits for working at firms in lieu of a salary. I never do that. If someone is going to work for me, I'm going to pay that person a fair wage. Why? I want them incentivized to do good work. Anyone working for no wage has less incentive to excel.

I understand self-motivation and pride in work, but when it comes to putting in that extra effort, like working that extra half-hour beyond 5:00 to finish an important task, if there's no financial incentive, that person is out the door. Are there exceptions to that? Of course. But that's our policy. I also believe it's a better, more meaningful experience for the student. Let them start seeing their value to a firm. Let this experience represent the floor of their legal compensation history. You gotta start somewhere. Everyone needs a benchmark.

Per Diem

The next step up in attorney staffing is utilizing *per diem* people. Tons of attorneys out there do *per diem* work. COVID-19 may affect their relevance as court appearances and conferences go video. We'll see how far that goes.

Regardless, you can find someone for almost anything: signing up cases, covering court appearances, doing depositions, writing motions or appeals, etc. What you may give up with a *per diem* worker is quality. Not that they're bad attorneys. Most are very good. But for them, it's a one-day connection to a case. They don't know your clients. They're not familiar with the intricacies of the case. They don't feel the same sense of obligation and emotion towards the case as you or your employees. In a one-day assignment, there's little accountability.

On the other hand, they may save you an entire day! That's worth something! It comes down to a cost/benefit analysis. Is the *per diem* saving you more than they cost? For me, they're terrific for mundane, inconsequential tasks. We use them for routine court appearances and discovery motions. If I can keep an employee in the office for three hours in the morning doing important paperwork to move a case forward vs. attending a nonsense compliance conference, call in the *per diem*!

It's actually very easy. In New York, each borough has regular *per diems* whose entire practices are based on making these kinds of court appearances for firms like mine. They are familiar with the local courthouse, judges, and court personnel. They spend every morning shuffling between all the courtrooms on behalf of multiple attorneys who utilize their services.

Be careful! Any matter that requires detailed knowledge about a case or specific discovery requests or important motions may not be suitable for a *per diem*. Not that they can't do it; but if it involves an esoteric, important issue or requires detailed knowledge of the facts and history of the case, you want to send someone with intimate familiarity with the case. Just be smart about it!

Of Counsel

The term "Of Counsel" means different things to different firms, but basically, it's a relationship with someone who may work in your office a few days per week or month or provide a service to you on a recurring basis. The advantage of this kind of setup is that it's not a full-time employee for whom you have to pay a salary plus benefits.

My firm has gotten pretty creative with this one. As our caseload has grown, so have the motions and appeals. Those are big time-consuming tasks for my business. Even though many of the issues we address repeat, every case is different, and the facts always change. To free up my attorneys and allow more productivity, we hired an Of Counsel appellate attorney to prepare appeals and draft the heavy motions. She comes to the office once a week and charges us a flat fee for her services. What's more, she's available to consult in the office. She's terrific on the law and contributes tremendously to case strategy and trial tactics. She's worth every penny!

We've also tapped a valuable resource previously untapped in our field: retired attorneys! Three recently retired attorneys work 1-3 days a week as Of Counsel. These gentlemen were atop the legal field in their heyday. Each has a wealth of knowledge and experience relevant to our specific and specialized practice. More importantly, all were defense lawyers in our field, which provides incredibly valuable insight we never had before. We're now a plaintiffs' firm with defense attorney staffers. That's genius!

These guys give us the perspective to really explore all the issues from intake through trial. They help with the biggest variable on our cases: value. What's the case worth? We often struggle with this question. They've valued cases over their entire careers, from the other side. So, what's my process with them on valuations? I ask their opinions, triple their numbers, and that's my demand on the case!! ☺

I even incentivize each of these Of Counsel guys differently. One works strictly hourly; another is solely commission (he works only on settling cases and gets a set percentage of each settlement), and the other is a hybrid. That's a great example of using your employees' assets and individual skill sets for the firm's benefit. Pay attention, people! This is good stuff. Not to toot my own horn, but the New York Law Journal even featured this aspect of our practice as new and innovative.

My advice: Start delegating as soon as it's warranted. There's a psychological element to it for you solos. You tend to hold out until it's absolutely necessary to hire. Nonsense! The sooner you recognize you need help, get it! That will free you up to focus your attention on the important stuff and facilitate growth. Finding a great worker can be a godsend!

Connie Chapter Six

TAKE CARE OF YOU FIRST

Jeff's got great advice for staffing issues. All that stuff about *per diem* and Of Counsel makes sense. That sounds awesome! Especially if you speak Latin.

But I don't speak Latin. I also don't speak Spanish, even though I'm Argentinian!! I speak about being happy and loving life, my own universal language. I'm more concerned about YOU rather than anyone you may or may not hire. More importantly, YOU must be concerned about you and what makes you happy. If you're clear about what you want and what you need in your business (and in your life!), then the staffing issues will take care of themselves. If you take care of YOU, everything else falls into place.

What do I mean? Focus on what you want. Contemplate and visualize your goals, big and small. You want a big firm? Cool. You want a small one? That's cool, too. You want a specific niche practice? Bigger? National reach? Global? They're all good – if that's what you want.

Once your vision is clear and you believe in it 100%, all the staffing issues resolve themselves. You simply continue making decisions that serve your goal and vision. It's that simple.

y only caution: Don't grow too early. While your goals may be limitless, your wallet may have some limits, at least early on.

My best advice: Grow when you can afford to. Don't put yourself in debt just to compete with bigger firms. Just as clear goals have importance, so does being financial savvy. Dream big but spend smart.

And don't let anyone work for free. While it may be tempting to accept an offer from some student to "volunteer" for you to "just to get some experience," that's never ideal. Jeff mentioned this, but my take is a bit different. If someone is looking to invest time in your firm, you should at least invest in them. You are running a business. Value the people that are helping you fulfill your goals and dreams, even if it's just minimum wage. It's the right thing to do and you (and that person) will feel better for it.

JEFF CHAPTER SEVEN

MANAGING/SUPERVING PEOPLE

You grew your firm and have a staff. Congratulations. You're a manager! What did they teach you in law school about that? Again: probably nothing.

Managerial and supervisory skills have nothing to do with what law school teaches. Courses do exist, but that's in business school. Law schools have shifted from a 100% classroom education, offering wonderful programs that provide exposure to real-life work experience. Every law student should take advantage of those. But as a student intern or clerk, you are (hopefully) closely supervised and managed.

Transition To Manager

But back to you, boss. As the leader of your firm, it's your job to manage, supervise, nurture, mentor, motivate and discipline your staff, including non-lawyers. How do you do it? If you have no experience, you read a book like this one! Hello??!!

For me, I thought the transition from worker to supervisor would be simple. I was a "leader" in many aspects of my life. From sports, to student government, to schoolwork, I often became the leader of the group. For the office I thought, "No problem."

But it was definitely a transition. Why? I realized that in the past, I mostly led by example. I most often would let my actions, on the field or in the classroom or within a group, speak for me. I gained people's respect by my actions and they followed my lead. In the office, well ... not so much.

I found it challenging to transition from employee/co-worker to partner/boss of former co-workers. Those same people I commiserated with, I now managed and supervised. It changed in one day! With very little notice! And absolutely no training! On Friday morning, it was "Hi, Jeff" and on Monday, it was "Morning, boss." It felt weird. I wasn't that comfortable with it.

Why? My personality. As much as I love trial work and advocating for clients inside the courtroom, outside the courtroom I avoid conflict. That seems strange for someone who wanted to be a lawyer since high school, but it's true. I'm not a big debater in my private life. I don't love fighting over issues. I don't enjoy political banter at holiday dinners. I'm not a screamer or a yeller. I like being vocal about happy, fun things (with Connie!). I want everyone to get along and smile and laugh.

So how in the world do I love being a trial lawyer? There's an important distinction. The conflicts in court are controlled. They are expected. I can prepare for them. I know my issues. I understand my arguments. I pretty much know my adversary's issues and arguments. And most importantly, there's a judge. Whatever the conflict, there's a neutral, uninterested person officiating all this, putting each issue to bed. Sure, these decisions may be appealable, but for the time being, they're over. That feels good to me. In court, an issue arises, we make our arguments, a decision is made, and we move on. Beautiful. Let's keep going. Call the next witness, counselor. I love it.

But that Monday morning I showed up as the boss and everything changed. As a manager and supervisor, I didn't know what issues would arise. I wasn't prepared to handle them. There was no arbitrator or process for dealing with them. Essentially, I was the judge and jury for everyone and everything.

In the office, no skilled advocates made arguments before me. I had people and personalities from extremely different lives, backgrounds, experiences, cultures, all with different moods, habits, personalities, quirks, needs, and levels of maturity. I managed everyone: people I really liked as co-workers, people I didn't, and others I didn't really know at all. But I was expected to treat everyone fairly and consistently. No favorites, no biases. Just evenhandedness.

That was tough and still is. Don't get me wrong, I love being the boss. I love the freedom, rewards, perks, and everything else it brings. But I still don't love the conflicts. I don't love the discipline part. I often feel forced to interact more with the people I don't enjoy, since they require more oversight, supervision, and discipline. But I would never trade in being the boss.

So how does all this apply to you? Here's my advice: Let's get back to the Kumbaya moment where you ask yourself, "Who am I? What's my personality? What are my comfort skills? What comes easy? What makes me feel queasy?" Whatever the answers, you can be a good boss. Just come to terms with the job requirement, accept it, welcome it with open arms, and work at it. You can do it!

Practical Tips:

Enough with the group life-coaching session (sorry, Connie). Here are some practical tips for managing and supervising people.

Create The Right Culture

As the boss and leader of the business, everything you do sets the tone for the office culture. Create an atmosphere that's fun, pleasant, and congenial, while at the same time it is professional. Gain the respect of the employees as a serious, hard-working leader, yet compassionate about their feelings, perceptions, and total experience as a cog in the wheel of your company.

What does that mean? Just be yourself! There's no magic switch to flip when you go from employee to boss or solo practitioner to employer. Just continue being who you are. You grew to this point for a reason – whatever you're doing is working!

It's simply a matter of treating people with respect and expecting respect in return. Say good morning to everyone when you come in. Say goodnight when you leave. Engage in conversation at the coffee machine. Have a real interest in everyone's personal life – learn and remember something about what's going on in their lives outside the office. Talk about TV shows, movies, family stuff, hobbies, etc.

If you're funny, then be funny. But you need to enforce the company policies and address issues quickly and efficiently. The staff must know that your policies and procedures are real and must be followed. They must know that certain failures warrant some kind of consequences. It's not necessarily "fear" to instill; merely an understanding that bad behavior will be called out and not tolerated. That's very important.

Communication Is Key

The most important component to any relationship is communication. The more the better. Every worker appreciates a clear understanding of their job description and the expectations of their managers and supervisors. Continued and repeated reinforcement of expectations is imperative! This may sound simple, but it's often overlooked and forgotten. It's easier to say nothing and hope behaviors change rather than confront things head on. Don't let that happen!

Feedback is critical. Employees need constant feedback. Without it, nobody knows if they're doing things right. This goes for positive *and* constructive feedback (I'm purposely not using the term "negative" feedback; that's not a helpful term). Both are equally important.

Positive feedback reinforces a job well done; constructive feedback clarifies your expectations and hopefully prevents future failings. If you don't tell people they're doing something wrong, they'll never stop.

This is no different from having a spouse/partner with an annoying habit of burping out loud. If that's disgusting and bothersome to you, say something. If you don't, it will never stop and grow to annoy you more as time goes on. It's the like the pebble in your shoe: If you ignore the minor irritation it causes and leave it, eventually it breaks the skin, causes and open wound, gets infected and becomes a dangerous problem requiring medical attention. Maybe even an amputation! Small communication issues grow into big ones that seriously affect relationships. Your office relationships are no different.

Meetings work, too. Some offices work well with informal meetings that develop naturally throughout the day. Issues arise, attorneys naturally gather to discuss, and a meeting begins! That's great.

But formal, scheduled meetings are important as well. How often? It really depends. In my practice, I encourage my attorneys to meet with their teams every week. A rotating agenda covers very specific areas. This keeps the meetings mostly short and sweet. At the same time, the attorneys meet every Wednesday to discuss strategy on larger cases, valuation, experts needed, etc. Schedule and hold meetings like these consistently. Video conferencing makes this easy.

What's a good meeting? It's really a culture and style decision for your firm. For me, a good meeting is scheduled with a clear agenda, distributed days before the meeting. Everyone gets an opportunity to consider the topics and details before the meeting.

My meetings rarely exceed one hour. I create an agenda that includes every participant in some way. As the meeting leader, I stick to the agenda and move the meeting along. My assistant records the minutes of the meeting.

These minutes, with the specific assignments meted out at the meeting, get recorded, documented, and distributed to everyone.

The next meeting starts with the tasks assigned at the prior meeting. Were they done? If not, why not? This reminds everyone that the decisions made at each meeting are meaningful. Tasks were created and expectations set. If the work wasn't done, there better be a good explanation.

Motivate The Right Way

I used to think that money is the best motivator. Why? That always motivated me! But I've learned that not everyone thinks and feels the way I do. In fact, most people don't! It's taken me very long to accept that not everyone is like me: determined to work hard, be the best and become the boss someday. Most people have lower expectations for themselves, they simply don't want the hassle or responsibility, or they just aren't interested. Some people just want to have a job to pay their bills and find enjoyment and satisfaction from other things in life.

But you can always start with money. What's the first question asked about a job? What's the salary! And what does everyone want every year? A raise! What else? A bonus! All those are money. Money is generally a great motivator. But how?

Raises And Bonuses

We used to determine raises and bonuses in December of every year over lunch at a diner. Our scientific method consisted of reviewing last year's raises and bonuses and asking each other, "Did we have a good year?" If so, we'd give a little more than last year. If not, we'd give a little less. Done! And I'll have gravy-cheese fries on the side with that!

Sounds easy enough, but not very satisfying for the staff. A better approach ties compensation and bonuses to the success of the business in a very specific and meaningful way. How? I know a business with an interesting approach:

This business created a structured system based on the gross profits of the firm. They set an annual gross income goal for the firm. If the goal is reached, the staff receives a bonus of 5% of their base salary. If $1 million in income exceeds the goal, the bonus is 7.5%. If $2 million exceeds the goal, it's 10%, and so on. By the same token, if they're short by half a million, they get only a 2.5% bonus. If they are short more than that, it's zero. Now that's clear!

What's more, they keep a white board posted in the office with a running total of the year's gross income, updated weekly. Everyone passing by knows exactly what track they are on, whether it's to meet the goal, exceed it, or if they are short. It's a daily reminder of what's important to the business: making money. Nice!

Money motivates many, but not all. Some seek a simple "good job" from the boss. A little positive reinforcement can go a long way. You'd be surprised how meaningful a few kind words of encouragement or approval can go. Some people just want to be appreciated for all the work they put into their job. Make a point of noticing that.

Utilize People's Strengths

Identifying your employees' strengths is key. Just because someone's a lawyer, doesn't mean she can try cases, write briefs, or communicate with clients, or bring in business. Your job is to recognize and understand everyone's strengths and utilize them for the benefit of the firm (and for their own benefit and happiness).

Say you hire a great trial attorney and incredible rainmaker – a terrific combination, by the way! Assume this attorney gets most of her business on the golf course, where she's an 8 handicap (an excellent player). What if her staff complains that she's always late in completing motions, Bills of Particular, and other paperwork? What if it's true? What if it's clear that she just can't sit behind a desk for too long without getting antsy? Those "desk" functions contribute to the profitability of the firm. Attacking the paperwork keeps the cases moving and ultimately gets them resolved sooner, bringing more money to the firm sooner. That's good for everyone. What to do with this attorney who can't effectively do the paperwork?

Take away her trials and prevent her from attending golf outings during the workweek? Put her behind a desk until she learns the importance of completing the paperwork timely? Will that teach her a valuable lesson? Of course not! That doesn't punish her, it punishes the firm.

Your job is to identify this. Consider other ways to get her paperwork done. It's not easy just to hire another attorney, so what else do you do? Be understanding about it. Talk to this attorney. Tell her how much you appreciate what she brings to the firm. Explain that the cases need to move and that the paperwork needs to be done. Perhaps a paralegal or other assistant could be of some help here. But don't punish her for having a limited skill set. Everyone has a limited skill set. Nobody can do everything well. Set up a system that utilizes everyone's skill set in a way that helps the firm most.

Discipline – Use A Handbook

This one is tough for some people (like me) and easier for others (like my partner). That's why we are great partners – our skills complement each other. Every supervisor and manager must discipline people at some point. If it doesn't come naturally, work on it. Practice it by role-playing with your partner. But like everything else, do it in a way that fits your personality. If I disciplined people the way my partner does, it wouldn't feel good to me and wouldn't be effective. It wouldn't be genuine.

The best way to establish disciplinary rules is with a company handbook. I know what you're thinking, solos: I'm not AT&T or Google. Why do I need a handbook? I only have two people working for me and they're part time!

But create one! It's not hard. Download something from the web. Anything. Read it and change it to fit your needs. It can be three pages if that's all you need. My point is you need something. Something official to the staff. Something tangible for them to read and sign (acknowledging that they read and understand it). Something that formalizes rules and protocols for the firm, including the disciplinary process.

Here's a sample Table of Contents for a handbook: (Figure 2)

YOUR SUCCESSFUL LAW FIRM

EMPLOYEE HANDBOOK

<u>TABLE OF CONTENTS</u>

12. LEAVE BENEFITS AND OTHER WORK POLICIES

    A. Holidays

    B. Vacation

    C. Sick Leave

    D. Personal Leave

    E. Military Leave

    F. Jury Duty

    G. Parental Leave

    H. Bereavement Leave

    I. Extended Personal Leave

    J. Severe Weather Conditions

    K. Meetings and Conferences

13. REIMBURSEMENT OF EXPENSES

14. SEPARATION

15. RETURN OF PROPERTY

16. REVIEW OF PERSONNEL AND WORK PRACTICES

17. PERSONNEL RECORDS

18. OUTSIDE MPLOYMENT

19. NON-DISCLOSURE OF CONFIDENTIAL INFORMATION

20. COMPUTER AND INFORMATION SECURITY

21. INTERNET ACCEPTABLE USE POLICY

Disciplinary Process

What's a disciplinary process? For my firm, there's an escalation system. If an issue arises, the manager simply talks to the people involved to get the lowdown. What happened? Who did what? If it's a misunderstanding, someone's having a bad day, personalities are conflicting, or it's something that doesn't violate firm policy, it's addressed, and we move on.

If someone violated company policy, there's a process:

1. The manager tells the offender what was done wrong and explains why that violates policy, detailing the correct behavior and what should have been done.

2. The manager documents the incident in writing (for the manager's own records).

3. If it happens again, meaning the bad behavior is repeated, the offending employee is "written up." The manager drafts a memo detailing the events, along with a warning of future consequences, if the behavior continues. Those consequences may include termination.

4. The employee reviews and signs this document and can comment in writing, giving their side of the events.

If the behavior occurs again, you now have solid support for a potential termination. Why? You put the employee on notice, in writing, that the behavior was improper and could result in termination. The issue escalates until the problem is rectified and behavior changes. If the employee can't change and the behavior persists, termination is supported by the documentation.

What's amazing about a system like this is that the situation often rectifies itself, without you terminating anyone. For the employee destined to remain with you, the behavior will change. For the employee who really isn't happy in the job but won't admit that to herself (or if she doesn't consciously realize it), this process is a reality check. It provides the impetus for the unhappy employee to leave on her own, which is the best outcome.

Change is good. Turnover is healthy. Not everyone is meant to stay at one job for life. It's not a failure when someone leaves. It's a new beginning and a fresh start, for the employee and for you. Whenever someone gives me notice, I congratulate them! It's usually a nerve-wracking experience for that person to enter the boss's office and quit. I'm never angry or upset. There's always a good reason why it's happening. Embrace it and move on. It's an opportunity for you to evaluate the remaining mix of your people and improve it. It's a win for everyone.

Reviews And Feedback

Before busting out the handbook and writing people up, ask yourself, "Is this going to be a surprise to Sally Sue?" If yes, then you didn't properly communicate or provide feedback to Sally Sue. People don't know you're unhappy with their performance unless you tell them. Many employees believe they're doing a bang-up job. They've set their own bar at a certain height and are hitting it every day! If you haven't told them otherwise, why should they think any differently?

Address things as they happen. Big and little things. If you see someone on a cell phone, say something. You don't need to yell "gotcha" and snatch the phone from their hands. You don't ever want to make a scene in the office. Simply ask, "Is everything alright?" They'll usually respond quickly with a "sure" and hastily put away the phone. If that's a continuing problem (which it is in many offices), bring the person into your office and talk about it. Tell them you asked if everything was alright because they're not supposed to be on their cell phone. Remind them of the policy in the firm. Of course, if that keeps happening, the discipline needs to be escalated.

But have the simple conversation first. There's no need for yelling or screaming. If someone drafts a motion with many mistakes, tell him. Make the changes and explain why they were necessary. Stress the importance of quality work.

I tell everyone that the firm's reputation is everything. We don't advertise. We get most of our clients from referrals. If sloppy correspondence on our letterhead is sent to clients or attorneys, that's a reflection of the firm's competence. That affects our reputation, which affects the business. My goal is not to stress out anyone, but to educate them on the importance of quality work product.

We provide formal, annual reviews to all employees. There's a formal write-up and an in-person meeting. Employees are encouraged to participate and provide their own written input into the report. The process is a bit labor-intensive, but I think it's important.

Everyone needs some kind of feedback, positive or constructive. The annual review is ok, but if you don't do periodic informal reviews or provide critical and useful feedback throughout the year, you won't remember what happened.

We keep employee files on everyone, for the good and the bad. Feedback isn't just for screwups! Praising people works wonders! Point out the good stuff. Congratulate great results. Send a firm-wide email heaping praise on good work. Post wins on your social media platforms. Recognize and publicize successes for everyone, not just attorneys. Keeping your good workers happy is more important than disciplining bad behavior; and it's a lot more fun to do. Your good people need to feel good. They need to know you appreciate their skills and talents. Tell them that!

My advice: Just treat everyone the way you want to be treated. If someone didn't like what I was doing, I would hope they'd tell me right away. If I were in a relationship with someone for years and found out she never liked the smell of my deodorant, I'd be mortified. Why didn't you tell me sooner? I would have switched brands! What if I hated the new pillows that she bought for the bed 2 years ago because they were uncomfortable? If I kept my mouth shut, I'd have a stiff neck for 2 years. That doesn't feel good! The same is true in the office. You need to break the silence on issues and communicate.

Connie Chapter Seven

BE THE SAME YOU - ALWAYS

If you're the boss, it happened for a reason. You set the goal, went for it, and got it. Congrats! You've grown to where you have a staff. Congrats, again! Now you need advice on how to manage and lead people?

No, you don't! Just be YOU! You became a leader by being a leader. Keep it going, girl, (or dude)! You obviously have what it takes. You had the confidence to get this far. You achieved a lofty goal. Why change? You don't have to, and you shouldn't.

Just because your title has changed doesn't mean you should. The notion that elevation to boss (or any position) comes with new responsibilities requiring you to become someone else is just wrong. You should NEVER be or act like someone you aren't. That's what screws up people. You don't need to be someone different, depending on your audience. Find yourself. Find your voice. Find your personality. Find your comfort zone. That's you. No matter where you are or who you're talking to. That's the real you. Own it.

The juggling of your different personalities is unhealthy and exhausting. Waking up with your spouse, being happy and funny in the morning, and then arriving at work only to morph into Mrs. Cranky-pants won't feel good! Nobody likes Mrs. Cranky-pants. Unless you truly are Mrs. Cranky-pants all the time (which may be something you need to work on – call me!).

Don't think of employees as your "staff" or "workforce" or "subordinates." They're PEOPLE! People you hired to help you achieve your goals and dreams. People you invested in to hop on your boat and set sail towards the promised land. People you trust with managing your affairs, speaking with your clients, and spending your money. Love these people!!! If you do, they'll love you back. *It's a give and take situation.* The employer/employee relationship is just that – a relationship. And like any relationship, it requires communication, cooperation, compromise, listening, under-standing, and nurturing.

I know, I know. You're now going through all your previous and current coworkers in your mind, thinking how much you DON'T love them at all. How this one's a jerk, the other one's a gossip, that one maybe reeks (his spouse didn't tell him about his deodorant) and this other one is just a miserable person. I get it.

But think about your real family. Do you connect with everyone on the same level? Do you have that favorite (or least favorite) aunt, uncle, or cousin? Are you closer with one sibling more than the other? Is one of your parents easier to talk to? You, see? That's what I'm talking about. You still love those family members because they're your family. That's the kind of love I'm talking about for your employees. You should appreciate them for their commitment to you and your firm. When you embrace yourself for being YOU, you must be open to accepting others being THEM.

Oh, man! I'm hearing Jeff's voice in my head now. "It's a business! They're not family! You can't fire your family! What are you talking about?"

I am not suggesting you adopt these people into your family. I am getting you into the mindset of an effective leader and boss. If you approach the relationship correctly, the decisions you make will be easy. Employees want a confident leader, clear guidance, understandable direction, and timely feedback. Jeff loves real life examples. Here's what I mean:

Instill Confidence

If you hire someone, have confidence they'll be a good employee. Why else did you hire them? They need to know that. They need to hear that. It's your job to inspire them.

On day one, tell them why they were hired, where they fit in the big scheme of the firm, and exactly how they will add to the firm's success. Give them the big picture. Explain the business to them. Every person, including the receptionist, mail person, file clerk, secretary, and intern should understand what the firm does and how it makes money. Knowledge and understanding equals power. You need to empower all your employees. Make them feel part of something big.

Set Expectations

There's a reason you create positions for employees. Each job fulfills a critical function of the firm, whatever it may be. Every employee should be clear about their position, responsibilities, and expectations. Don't let the job title tell the story.

Job titles have different meanings in different firms. Ideally, employees should have a written job description of their duties, responsibilities, and expectations. If you're not that formal, just tell them! Communication is essential to any relationship. The beginning of any relationship sets the tone. Be clear with what's expected from each position. Start every employee off right.

Provide Feedback

Give lots of positive-influenced feedback often. For good stuff and bad stuff. This may be tough for some bosses, but it's critical to the business. Many type-A people (who often become bosses) struggle with feedback. Their thought process generally is, "Nobody had to tell me what to do; I didn't need a pat on the back to motivate me; I didn't care what anyone thought; I just did my job." All that may be true.

But understand this: Your employees aren't you. That's *really* important so I'm going to say it again: Your employees aren't you. Don't assume they have the same drive, desires, goals, aspirations, expectations, or perspective you had on your way up the ladder. Most of them will never get to where you are. Many of them don't want to. Stop trying to figure out what they really want. Just be clear about what you want and continuously reinforce that to them. How? By recognizing their good efforts and behavior and calling out what needs improvement.

The positive stuff is easy to convey. It's generally easier to compliment than criticize (for most people). And it doesn't have to be an event. You don't need to stop the workday to announce that Sally Sue did well and hang a medal around her neck. Just give her a quick "nice job" or "good work" when deserved. Even a quick email recognizing her efforts is fine. For many employees, any kind words from the boss go a very long way.

The negative stuff is typically harder. But it shouldn't be. Just don't be a jerk about it. Every misstep taken by an employee is an opportunity for you to develop that person. That's the way to look at it! It's a chance for you to set your expectations, remind them of how their job fits into the big picture, and emphasize the ultimate goals of the firm. Those are teachable moments.

Talk to them the same way you hoped someone talked to your younger, inexperienced self if you made the same mistake. Then let it go, unless of course if it keeps coming up. At which point you may question whether this person is the right fit for this position. It doesn't mean they are a "bad" worker. It may mean that their strengths are best suited for a different position. Remember, nobody is meant to be great at everything. But everyone does have something they are great at. Maybe they are not in the right job.

Never Scream

Don't blow up when you're upset (perhaps like your mother or father did to you). If that's what you experienced at home or in a prior work environment, disconnect the chain, break that cycle. Why did it bother you? Because it sucks to be yelled at! It's not nice, it doesn't feel good and it discourages as opposed to motivates. Hello?

Speak to employees the way you like to be spoken to; the way you wanted your boss to treat you when you were in that position. Always remember what it was like to be an employee. There is NEVER a reason to be a jerk. You're a leader. It's your role and responsibility to act like one.

Be Open

Just because you're the boss doesn't mean you're always the smartest person in the room. Everyone has skills and assets they bring to the table. As a leader, it's your job to identify those skills and use them to advance the firm. Employees often know more than you about the "subculture" of the firm, meaning what's going on outside your office. They may also understand the business better than you think they do. Their thoughts and ideas can be extremely useful. Listen to them.

Create an environment and forum for the workers to express their thoughts and ideas. Welcome and encourage this. I guarantee you'll hear things you never would have known or considered. Even if you don't, it's important to your staff that they be heard. Sometimes the quiet ones have the best ideas. Unless they have an avenue to share (and some encouragement), those ideas remain unspoken.

What kind of "environment" or "forum" am I talking about? Just talk to them! When someone comes into your office with a question, just ask them what *they* think about the issue. When you're waiting for a meeting to start, chitchat with the people in the room. Ask them questions about their lives and their families. Be a person! It's not really any harder than that.

Show Appreciation

This is a kind of positive feedback, but it needs to be specific. It's one thing to conduct a meeting and end it with, "… and I appreciate all that everyone does for the firm." It's quite another to pull someone into your office on Monday and tell that person, "I appreciate that you stayed late Friday night to finish that project. Because of your dedication, we will settle that case sooner." Comments like that, reinforcing and complimenting great work, motivates employees to perform at their best and confirms their positive contributions to the firm.

The take-aways here? *Be a happy, positive, inspiring leader first* – be the example. If you exude positive energy and don't make a big deal of little things, your people will follow your lead. Recognize the teachable moments, avoid criticizing, and instead DEVELOP. Embrace the role and be true to yourself! If you love and appreciate your people, your people will love you back! It's that simple.

Jeff Chapter Eight

OFFICE SPACE

A growing firm means more space is needed. Many solos start in a home office or a modest rental. When do you make that move to bigger space? And where do you go? Stay local or head into the big city? Cost is always a factor, but lifestyle is important, too. Where are you in your career? What's best for the business of the firm? What's best for you personally?

The impact of the COVID-19 pandemic on office space needs cannot be underestimated. Maybe you don't need so much space. Maybe you and your staff can work remotely and split time in the office. Maybe the physical office isn't as important as it used to be. While the need for actual space may decrease, I believe lawyers will still need professional office space. We'll see!

What's the old saying about the three most important factors in real estate? Location, location, and location. It's important for any business. The decision for you to make is, at what cost?

My firm was in lower Manhattan for over 25 years. For most of that time, I commuted by train from Long Island. As an early person, I was up at 5:15 a.m., on the 6:08 a.m. train and at my desk by 7:30 a.m. (7:15 if my subway connection was perfect). For me, those first 2 hours alone in the office were the most productive. No calls, no questions, no interruptions. But I didn't leave the office generally until about 7:00 p.m. That meant I was home by 8:30 p.m. I loved what I was doing, but those were long days.

Being in the city was important to me at that time. I joined 2 local Bar Associations and was very active in both, joining committees and attending functions. For one of them, I eventually sat on the board of directors! I often lectured to lawyers on trial practice and techniques. I was husting. It was fun. The city is an exciting place. The energy on the streets and in the office was truly palpable. It was great for my business, my career, and me.

But things eventually shifted. We opened a satellite office on Long Island. One of our largest referral firms (that concentrates in workers' compensation, social security, and disability cases) asked us to work as their "in house" personal injury department. It was a great fit, so we placed a couple of attorneys and staff there. Over time, the needs and business in that office grew. When our 10-year lease in the city office ended, we had to decide: stay in NYC or head out to Long Island. For us, it was time to go. For me, it was a life-changer. My commute went from 3 hours each way to 3 minutes each way. Everything in my personal life changed, for the better. The timing, and the costs, were right for me and my firm.

What Should You Pay For Rent?

There's no fixed rule for what percentage of business income your rent should be. Different industries set different standards – anywhere from 2 to 20 percent. Calculating the percentage is simple enough: Divide annual rent by anticipated revenue. For law firms, it's generally safe to be in the 5 to 7 percent zone. The ratio doesn't outweigh your individual situation, though: If you can't afford the first month's rent, it doesn't matter how good the rate is.

Do your own calculation. Take your firm's gross income and multiply it by the appropriate percentage for your type of business. If your gross annual income is $500,000, multiply this amount by 6 percent. This equals $30,000 (or $2,500 per month), which means this is the amount you "should" pay for rent every year.

The "post-pandemic" real estate market may drastically change. These percentages may need some adjustment, but the principles are the same.

Every situation is different. The importance and value of your space depends on lots of things. A personal injury firm (like mine) has clients visiting the office. They should be impressed, right? Especially if they're shopping their case around, meeting with several lawyers before deciding on the one. The office space and the initial meeting will certainly have an impact.

For an insurance defense firm, the clients are insurance companies. Rarely those clients will visit the office; most of the communication is by phone or correspondence. In that case, the office "visual" is less important. If the client doesn't care where your office is or how it looks, maybe you don't have to care so much. In the end, the less money spent on rent, the more is available for other things (like salaries and advertising), and to keep for yourself.

Where To Set Up Shop?

The decision to move is a very personal one. What are your goals? What are your needs? What are your priorities? What is your gut telling you? What will make you most happy?

Let's say you're ready to move. Wherever you're going, city or suburbs, get a commercial real estate broker. Don't do this alone. It's not a good use of your time. These days, brokers have all the information you need. They'll put everything in a beautiful, color binder with all the specifications you need to consider on each property.

Don't tell a broker you want to be on "Long Island." Narrow it down as much as possible. Pick a county. Pick a couple of areas. Otherwise your head will spin. Brokers want to show you many properties. That takes time, so be specific about properties that truly interest you. When visiting a site, take your own pictures and jot down notes. After seeing more than 3 places, you'll forget what you saw and what you liked about each place.

These days on Long Island, lots of space is available (a "renter's market"). Another COVID-19 residual! That means proprietors may offer some incentives up front to get you in the space. Find out exactly what that means in each building and who pays for what. Generally, the property owner should "build out" the space to your liking, within some boundaries. Know what you want. An open floor plan was the latest rage, until the pandemic hit. Now everything has changed. Big offices for the lawyers? Kitchen area? Conference rooms? File space? Reception area design? All things to consider.

Reception Area

Don't gloss over the reception area design. That's arguably the most important space for law firms. First impressions are so important! What's the first thing clients experience when visiting your office? The reception area. And sometimes they're sitting there for quite some time before meeting the attorney. They need to be comfortable. They need to be impressed. Give them an experience reassuring their decision to choose you as their attorney.

Is there a spot to hang coats or place umbrellas? Any coffee, water, or snacks? Where's the bathroom? What's there to read? How comfortable are the chairs? Are they given information about the firm's bio, history, and successes? Are any awards, accolades, or informational pamphlets about the firm displayed? Is there a television to watch? Who has the remote control? What's on the screen? A regular channel or a promotional video about the firm on a loop? What's the average wait in there for a client? Is the area clean? Please keep the area clean!

And perhaps most important: Who is the receptionist? That person is the first face seen by the client. How does the receptionist greet them when they arrive? Is it, "Have a seat," without looking up from the computer? Or is it a happy, smiling face with an energetic, "Welcome to the best firm in New York! How can we help you today?"

Once you're moved in and the dust has settled, take the time to experience exactly what a new potential client does. Drive up to the building or walk in from the street. What do you see? Is it impressive? Does it convey competence, excellence, and success? What type of signage is there? Would someone arriving for the first time know exactly where to go? Ensure that the first encounter with your firm is a positive, professional, comfortable, easy, and smooth experience. That first impression will last for a long time.

My advice: It's important to feel comfortable in your office. Think of your office as an extension of your home, not a place where you work, work, work, work, work. You should love your office, your desk, your chair, pictures, computer … everything! It should be a place you look forward to. Whatever your budget is, spend what you need to achieve this mindset. You'll be happier. Just ask Connie.

Connie Chapter Eight

LOVE WHERE YOU WORK

The goal is to make money, right? Never forget it's a *business* you're running. You must be very strategic with your spending. I say this from personal experience. When I first started my business, I spent wayyyyy more money than I should have. So many of my business "friends" were giving me advice on how to spend my money and I just didn't know any better. I spent a lot of money on things that weren't necessary, such as:

Networking groups (when there are plenty of free and low-cost ones)

Websites (now you can build your own)

Trademarks* (you can do this yourself online)

Business Cards/Marketing Materials (hello, Vistaprint)

And so on…

Don't do the same. It's not necessary when you're starting out, and the goal is for you to *make* money, not spend it.

In the beginning, you want your overhead to be low. Nothing is worse than being excited to start your new business, only to be overwhelmed by the stress of finances. Do yourself a favor: Start REAL cheap!

Don't think you have to appear bigger than you are. With that mindset, you actually hold yourself back. That thinking makes you believe you're competing with the bigger firms. Guess what? In the beginning, you can't. These firms have BIG budgets and BIG reputations. That's not you, YET. So, don't compare yourself to them and instead *create your own personalized "boutique" type firm with a specific niche.*

Check Your Money Status

Are you starting this biz on a wing and a prayer? Or do you have a savings that will cover your living/personal expenses until you start making money? Again, this matters. You don't want to be stressed. I've heard how some people use "stress" as motivation to get a business going, but that's really the hard way to go about it. You want the start of your business to be planned, smooth, and easy. Some ideas on how to keep it budget-friendly and simple include:

1)   Work from home

This avoids the expense of rent altogether. If you need to meet clients (and you don't feel comfortable doing it at home), you can always rent office space by the hour or day at a local shared workspace. They're popping up everywhere now.

If you do set up a home office, be sure you love it and it inspires you. Instead of spending money on rent, use that money to update your home office. This space reflects you and your success. Paint it a color that inspires you. Furnish it with your style and taste. Keep it organized and ready for business.

Often as I begin to work with clients in their home office, I'm surprised at the lack of "love" in the room. Usually it's the odd room in the house with scattered piles of unrelated work items. Or it's not decorated at all. Just plain. This is not a good representation of the business you want, even if you're the only one seeing it. Your home office should remind you of all the reasons you love what you do and why you do what you do. Because once you have your own business, you're going to be in that office a lot!

COVID-19 forced the whole country to work from home. Everyone learned video conferencing (Zoom, Skype, Facetime, etc.) real fast, even judges and Boomers! This is an enormous win for business starters. Just set up your video shot with some fancy-shmancy office props in the background (and lose the pajamas). Potential clients, adversaries, and judges won't know the difference!

2) *Add music*

Everyone loves music! For me, I've had a wireless speaker in all my offices. I LOVE streaming Pandora's coffee house playlists. It's easy listening and I keep it low as I work (but not while I write since that requires a different level of concentration 😊). It lightens up the place and my mood while working on projects.

When I work with clients one-on-one, I also listen to music but in a different way. I know weird, right? Currently I work out of our home and see clients in person. For me, the choice is convenience and I LOVE the comforts of working out of the house. That may change, but for now, that's what I love.

In the house, on our main TV downstairs I blare today's pop music from a TV music channel. My office is located upstairs in the far corner of the house. I do this because when I meet with clients, it's all about upbeat, positive, forward-motion sessions. Welcoming clients with fun music in the background sets the right mood. It beats the typical, quiet, boring entrance to an office. Plus, I just love it! And where my office is located, you hear the music faintly with the door closed, which I love. It promotes a fun, happy environment, the way life is supposed to be! And the way my sessions are!

3) *Furniture - don't go nuts!*

As my girlfriend Jules always says, when you buy furniture (or clothes!), buy high/low. Mix a combination of low-end purchases (Ikea, Target, etc.) with high-end purchases (Pottery Barn or whatever is high for you). The goal is to keep it cost effective while still creating an environment that inspires you. Don't spend a lot on furniture since your taste may change as your business evolves. Buy what you love, but it doesn't have to be expensive.

When I rented my first office space many years ago, I purchased LOTS of barely used, nice, and cheap furniture on Craigslist. This was a huge win as a lot of the furniture was from businesses relocating or shuttering. It was a win-win. I got a deal and they were able to unload their stuff. This of course isn't for everyone, but it certainly worked for me at the time.

4) *Rent in a shared office space*

Why rent an entire space when you just need a room? Lots of buildings have shared suites where you only rent a room. This is more for those that don't have the space at home, don't want to work at home, or simply want to be around people.

For this, just *ensure the suite space reflects who you are.* As Jeff mentioned, the reception area or entrance to your office should be inviting and warm. It's the first impression your client gets, even if it's not your actual waiting room.

5) *Rent a reasonable office space*

This is the most expensive option, as it's usually a bigger space which often includes the additional costs of utilities. This would obviously be an option once you are financially ready and possibly have a staff. This space is a bit easier to revamp and decorate to reflect your business.

Remember, you are starting out. Don't go nuts. Make money first, look out for all your expenses, and then upgrade later. This will give you a sense of accomplishment.

JEFF CHAPTER NINE

INSURANCE

Hey, business owner! Have enough decisions to make so far? Should you start a business? What's your niche? Who to hire? How to manage everyone? Where to set up shop?

Here's a fun one: insurance! What kind do you need? How much should you get? OMG - when do all these decisions end??? Finally, this time the answer is not "it depends." For you, this answer is NEVER! Get used to it, people!

You make decisions every day. Running a business means making decisions. That's what the boss does. Don't complain about it. Be happy nobody is making decisions for you. Decision-making comes with independence. You control your own destiny. And don't beat yourself up for making the wrong decision about anything. If something doesn't work out, change it! No big deal. You surely learned something from whatever didn't work out. There's always a positive takeaway. (Oh my, I think I'm becoming Connie!). Find the positive in every experience and then move on. Tomorrow is always better!

Professional Liability (Malpractice) Insurance; Errors and Omissions

Back to insurance. It's an important topic. First and foremost, let's talk about Malpractice Insurance (also called "Professional Liability" or "Error and Omissions" coverage). You need it. How much depends on what you do. If you handle personal injury and medical malpractice cases like me, you need a lot. I'm bringing lawsuits seeking millions of dollars in damages (not just as a scare tactic – significant injuries warrant these kinds of payouts). But that means if I screw up the case and commit malpractice, the client can sue me. If that happens, I'm liable for compensating the client for the injuries I claimed the doctor caused! And I was seeking a ton of dough! Yikes! Doctors and medical facilities usually have coverage in the millions. You might need that, too.

So many areas of law are like minefields. Even the seasoned, veteran law firm can blow a statute of limitations due to "law office failure" (e.g. the paralegal entered the wrong accident date into the case management software program and then one day, kaboom!). Things like that can and do happen. But like I tell my doctors friends (which I do have), that's why you have insurance.

Take out enough coverage to protect against your biggest case, and then purchase an excess or umbrella policy. It's worth it. We all make mistakes. As your firm grows, you rely more and more on other people to work on your cases. You can't watch over everything. Malpractice insurance, like any insurance, helps you sleep better.

In today's world, Professional Liability coverage can be beefed up with enhancements to cover internet-related incidents. "Cyber" coverage offers protection against liability from accidentally sharing malicious software, data breaches, and other computer-related wrongful acts. Also, it safeguards your firm against losses, such as privacy breach notification costs, business interruption, forensic expenses, etc.

In addition, claims may arise because of damage to your documents or documents in your care, custody, or control (for my business, medical records). "Loss of Documents" coverage protects against cases of damaged documents. This enhancement covers the amount you become legally obliged to pay, including liability for the claimant's expenses.

General Liability Insurance

Of course, General Liability Insurance is needed, too. Just like the homeowners' insurance you have on your home, you need this, too.

General Liability Insurance (also called "Small Business Insurance" or "Commercial Liability Insurance") provides coverage against claims made for people injured or property damaged at the workplace (or offsite, while on the job). If someone comes to your place of business and is injured, a general liability policy would cover their medical costs, pain, and suffering. If someone else's property is damaged and you are found to be responsible, the repair or replacement cost could be covered. And if someone's reputation is damaged by something you or an employee said or wrote about them (defamation, libel), the associated costs could be covered.

As a small business owner, you may be legally responsible if another person gets hurt or if their property is damaged while at your business or because of something you did. You need to protect against these risks or accidents. They happen!

Workers' Compensation Insurance

But what happens if an employee is injured on the job? What if your paralegal's back goes out while she's pulling a huge file off the shelf? General Liability Insurance does NOT cover that accident. That's where Workers' Compensation coverage comes in.

Workers' Compensation Insurance provides cash benefits (money) and/or medical care for workers who are injured or become ill as a direct result of their job. Employers pay for this insurance and cannot require the employee to contribute to the cost of compensation. In New York, employers must have a workers' compensation insurance policy, unless your business is a sole proprietorship or a 2-person partnership or corporation. Since you're reading this book, you're probably bigger than that (or want to be!). Not every state requires this kind of insurance. Texas, for example, has no such requirement.

The workers' compensation system is like no-fault car insurance. Employees have a right to receive workers' compensation benefits for job-related benefits. The law requires employers operating in New York State to have workers' compensation coverage for employees, with limited exceptions. Employers are required to obtain and keep in effect workers' compensation coverage for all employees, even part-time employees and family members that are employed by the company.

Employment Practices Liability Insurance (EPLI)

(Sexual Harassment/Discrimination)

This is the new one! The #MeToo movement has spawned many things, including more insurance! Protecting against these kinds of claims is now essential. Educating your staff is a big part of this, too; it's now mandatory. Many states, including New York, require specific sexual harassment training, whether it be in person, by video, or some other way. Stay current! If you can afford this insurance, get it. This stuff is important, so I'm going to use bullet points to make it super-easy.

EPLI provides coverage to employers against claims made by employees alleging:

- Discrimination (based on sex, race, age, or disability);

- Wrongful termination;

- Harassment; and

- Other employment-related issues, such as failure to promote.

Large corporations typically have substantial EPLI coverage in place and are prepared to deal with just about any employment lawsuit. However, small or new businesses (like yours!) are often the most vulnerable to these claims. That's because they usually lack a human resources department or employee handbook detailing the policies and procedures that guide hiring, disciplining or terminating employees.

Here's a handy-dandy numbered list (in no particular order) of what you need to know and do:

1.   Review potential loss exposures with your insurance broker and consider EPLI coverage.

2.   Develop an employee handbook detailing your company's workplace policies and procedures, including attendance, discipline, and complaints. The employee handbook should also contain an employee "at-will" statement, which the employee must sign (see #6 below). The handbook should address your company's specific needs and can always be updated or amended. It should also include an equal opportunity statement.

Some cool, sample equal opportunity statements include:

From the U.S. Government: "The United States Government does not discriminate in employment on the basis of race, color, religion, sex (including pregnancy and gender identity), national origin, political affiliation, sexual orientation, marital status, disability, genetic information, age, membership in an employee organization, retaliation, parental status, military service, or other non-merit factors."

From Google: "At Google, we don't just accept difference — we celebrate it, we support it, and we thrive on it for the benefit of our employees, our products, and our community. Google is proud to be an Equal Opportunity Workplace and is an affirmative action employer."

From Facebook: "Facebook is proud to be an Equal Employment Opportunity and Affirmative Action employer. We do not discriminate based upon race, religion, color, national origin, gender (including pregnancy, childbirth, or related medical conditions), sexual orientation, gender identity, gender expression, age, status as a protected veteran, status as an individual with a disability, or other applicable legally protected characteristics. If you need assistance or an accommodation due to a disability, you may contact us at …"

3.   Create a job description for each position that clearly defines expectations of skills and performance.

4.   Conduct periodic performance reviews of employees and carefully note the results in the employee's file (oh, yeah – create employee files). Use employee files to keep track of the good and the bad. Celebrate good, creative, imaginative work with compliments and put copies in their files. Also, keep track of the bad stuff. If you don't, you won't remember any of it at year end when it's time for reviews and bonuses.

5.   Develop a screening and hiring program to weed out unsuitable candidates on paper before calling them to interview in person.

6.   Use an employment application for candidates that contains an equal employment opportunity statement, along with a statement that clearly states that, if hired, employment with be "at-will." This means their employment can be terminated at any time, for any reason or for no reason at all, with or without notice (but you still want processes in place that gives them notice and reasons, just so there are no surprises and because it's just the right way to conduct business – communication is key!). Also, ensure your employment application does not contain any age indicators, such as date graduated high school, since this could increase your risk for age discrimination claims.

7.   Conduct background checks on all possible candidates.

8.   Institute a zero-tolerance policy regarding discrimination, substance abuse and any form of harassment. Make sure you have an "open-door" policy in which employees can report infractions without fear of retribution.

9.   Create an effective record-keeping system to document employee issues as they arise. And add what the company did to resolve those issues.

A human resources (HR) consultant can certainly help with these issues. As my firm grew, we enlisted an HR consultant just to help create a handbook. She was so good we kept her on as a consultant! She gives us 1.5 days per week. If you can budget for this and you find the right person, it's worth every penny!

Directors And Officers (D&O) Insurance

This is probably not something high on the priority list, but I include it for completeness purposes. Directors and Officers (D&O) Insurance protects the personal assets of partners, corporate directors and officers, and their spouses, in the event they are personally sued by employees, vendors, competitors, investors, customers, or other parties, for actual or alleged wrongful acts in managing a company.

This coverage is NOT part of the General Liability coverage that most entities also purchase. It's also different from Professional Liability insurance or Errors and Omissions coverage. D&O covers *management decisions*. Professional liability covers malpractice of your business. A doctor cutting out the wrong kidney is professional liability. The board of the hospital might be sued for hiring the doctor that mistakenly cut out the wrong kidney – that's D&O.

D&O covers acts committed by a director or officer while acting within the scope of their duties. The acts covered generally apply to the large firms. Regardless, you should work closely with your insurance broker and discuss this option. You should explore all the areas of risks specific to your firm and each of the scenarios for which you could utilize management liability coverage.

Life Insurance

Life insurance is something everyone generally understands relevant to individuals. However, it can be a useful part of business strategy as well. Many partnership agreements include life insurance as payouts for the retirement or death of a partner. You can get creative with term, whole and universal policies to work out beneficial packages in the "what if" scenarios. It's something to consider.

Business Interruption Insurance

Business Interruption Coverage generally allows a business to recover certain losses if the business suffers physical damage or loss that prevents it from operating its business. This would generally include losses resulting from direct physical loss or damage to property caused by hurricanes, fires, wind damage, or theft. Does it cover losses caused by viruses or pandemics? Who knows? This coverage may also extend to losses and expenses resulting from a civil authority order, like a governor signing an Executive Order requiring everyone in the state to stay home (sound familiar?). Would that apply to the COVID-19 pandemic? Not sure yet.

By now, your head is spinning. It gets nuts! Additional available coverage includes (I'm not kidding): Kidnap Ransom and Extortion; Workplace Violence Expense; Alien Abduction Insurance; and even Lottery Insurance. What's Lottery Insurance? Well, what if your staff pools their money for the lottery and actually wins! Great, but what if they all quit the next day? This kind of insurance will cover the costs to find a new staff to replace the new millionaires. The list never ends!

My advice: Do you need all this coverage? It depends (ha ha!). It depends on what you need. What's your risk tolerance? What's your budget? What's likely to occur? When will the aliens get here? And be forewarned, people: It may come down to the persuasiveness of the insurance broker! Those people can be relentless!

Find someone you trust and break it all down. Don't fear the insurance issue. Embrace it! Make it fun. It gives you peace of mind.

Connie Chapter Nine

INVEST IN YOU

Insurance? What kind of topic is that? Insurance is preparing for problems, mishaps, and bad things. I don't do that. I think positive!! I only create good thoughts, not bad ones.

I'm kidding ... but the best insurance you can ever have is: YOU. Which means the only guaranteed investment is the one made in yourself and your future. By reading books like this and taking the necessary steps to develop YOU, you make your life better. That's the best insurance policy EVER. With a positive perspective in life, you can achieve and overcome anything. With that mindset, what more do you need?

Just take Jeff's advice on that other insurance stuff and you'll be fine. 😊

JEFF CHAPTER TEN

TECHNOLOGY

Technology is your best friend or your most frustrating enemy. I can't begin to say how wonderful technology advances have been for me; how they simplify my life and keep me more informed and efficient. At the same time, troubleshooting a technology issue is challenging. What happens when the electricity fails? When the computers are down? When the screen freezes? Everyone forgets how to write on a notepad, use a landline, and read actual documents!

The technology choices are endless and ever changing. Every two years, all my devices, subscriptions, and licenses become obsolete. Apple stops using disc drives, so the world no longer uses discs. Microsoft announces a new Word version, making my computers incompatible with the new software. The latest version of my case management software is now incompatible with the server it's running on. Do I need to jump to the cloud? Is that safe? Will my office information and client files fly up in the sky somewhere? How does that work? Is God looking through my cases? Where is everything?

Technology advances are not slowing down. Lots of people make lots of money as consumers just can't get enough of the latest and greatest stuff. Just accept it. You'll never be "up to date." You can only focus on what you need and what makes your business more efficient. Forget what everyone else is doing.

It's no longer an option. The COVID-19 pandemic has changed the technology landscape for lawyers. Before COVID-19, many lawyers begrudgingly acquiesced to the requirements of e-discovery and e-filing.

That's child's play, now! Lawyers originally complained about e-filing requiring documents to be digitized, moving everyone towards paperless options. Now? It's all about technology. Everyone, including the courts, have been forced to embrace a new normal, which includes video conferencing, Zoom, Skype, FaceTime, laptops, iPads, virtual mediations and arbitrations, e-notarizing, digital signatures, file sharing, cloud computing, backing up, storage, shredding … the list will continue to grow. The legal field (including the archaic court systems and courtroom configurations) will finally catch up with modern technology!

My best advice is this: Get a good IT person. Someone you trust. Someone who is looking out for your best interests. Someone who won't just spend your money because she wants the newest computer. The IT person is potentially worth as much as any attorney you hire (or more).

During the pandemic, my most valuable employee was my IT person. Without him, how would have everyone worked remotely? He purchased 25 VPN licenses (portals into the office computer system) two weeks before the shutdown. The fact that his relatives from Taiwan provided the "heads-up" about the coronavirus didn't hurt.

So Many Choices – What To Buy?

With so many IT choices, it's hard to prioritize. What's most important? What kind of technology can help you most? What kind will save you the most money?

Let's start small. My favorite gadget is my calendar. The switch from the pocket-sized black leather date book to the Outlook calendar was a game changer. With all its capabilities and options, having everything on my phone changed my world. But today, that seems far from extraordinary. There are a variety of digital calendars to choose from. Nowadays, I'm contemplating whether everyone in the office needs a desktop computer. Should they all be laptops? I don't know.

An important tech piece in my office today is the copy machine. Not because it just makes copies; it's everything else it does. My IT person configured all the settings to meet my specific needs, such as, no color copies without a password and case numbers assigned to each job so client files can be legitimately billed for the big jobs. Moreover, teaching everyone how to double-side copies and make four-sided, double sided copies with holes, so 1,000-page transcripts become 150-page transcripts that fit in a small binder. Anyone can configure a project's printing from their computer. All the potential combinations of one-sided, two-sided, four-sided, staples, hole punches, paper size, etc. are all one click away, before you go the printer to receive the document. That also saves time and backlogs at the machine. But of all the bells and whistles, the scanning capabilities are the most meaningful to me since that saves me money.

Scanning is really the future (which is now). But lawyers love paper. Lots of paper. Motions that contain 14 exhibits (including contracts and leases on 11x14 paper) just won't go away. Again, COVID-19 is quickly changing this. Up to now, the court systems have been mired in the Stone Age. Many New York State Courts still require paper copies of motions and submissions made to the court! This will soon change.

My office is now paperless. That conversion was a process. It's one thing to simply scan everything that comes in. It's another to point the scanner in the right place, label every document and store it in a place where everyone can find it. For that, the scanning person needs to think. Someone must read the document; know the case it pertains to, what to name the document, and exactly where to send it. What about responding or reacting to the document? The assigned attorney must know this document came in. You need a specialized system for all that. We're improving ours every day.

Trials And Technology

And what about trials? Don't get me started. The courtroom is the last venue for technological change. Manhattan's 60 Centre Street has a "courtroom of the future" which is where many medical malpractice cases are tried. What's the "futuristic" technology? A huge overhead projector for single page documents! I'm not joking. It's "futuristic" because there are monitors bolted into the jury box, witness box and in front of the judge and attorneys. That's progress?

The problem is that these court buildings are hundreds of years old. Each courtroom is configured differently. There is no "stage." Everything is "in the round," meaning that the lawyers face the judge, not the jury; the judge faces the lawyers, not the jury; the jury faces straight into nothing; the witness faces the back of the courtroom, not the jury; lawyers (when permitted) roam around the courtroom for drama and effect. Where are the exhibits and demonstrative evidence placed? Invariably, someone can't see what's going on. That's why the monitor-filled courtroom in Manhattan is so special. Everyone can see the exhibits from their seats, without shifting! Hallelujah!

The post-pandemic effects on the courtroom will be impactful. Since the courts have yet to resume trials (as I write this book), I can't say how. Stay tuned for the second edition!

Case Management Software

But let's get back to the office. The lifeblood of the office is the case management software. Choices abound, and they are all good. So good, that I think my firm is only using 25% of what our program can do. Not an efficient spend, but it's ok.

The trick is to get a program that caters to your specific needs. Every office operates differently: the way the calendar is managed, naming the tabs for separating documents, using templates for document forms, and the big one - what information goes into which box? Data entry is so important. These programs can do so many things, but they are all limited by the way the data is entered. If the data's not in there, or it's not in the right place, the system fails.

The toughest thing for me is getting everyone in the office to utilize the case management software consistently. Everyone needs to put the information in the same place! People tend to use the system to suit their individual habits and needs. Everyone has their own level of savvy, skill, and comfort with computer programs.

Just think, do Millennials use their phones the same way as Gen-Xers and baby boomers? Not a chance! Each generation has a different relationship with technology. And every person figures things out their own way. While it's good for the system to be flexible, you need to maintain uniformity so the data entered can be put to good use. Otherwise, the inputted data isn't helping everyone; it's only helping the person entering it.

You must stay on top of people and institute rules and protocols regarding data input. For this, you need to TRAIN the staff. Either someone from the software company or someone in the office needs to periodically provide "refresher" courses for everyone, just to ensure consistency. Make the program work for you.

Most case management software programs are now "mobile." They have apps for smart phones. Much of the information in the system can be accessed from outside the office through these apps. That's progress! Imagine being in court, conferencing a case with a judge, and your adversary insists that you did not provide some discovery document. Because you can't bring the whole file to court, you don't have the proof to show you sent it. Now, with the case management software app, you can access the correspondence in seconds. That's cool.

As I run the business, my most useful tool is the financial and case-related metrics and statistics capabilities of the case management software. So long as the data is entered correctly, I can acquire very useful information and even measure performance. I created metrics to tally each attorney's caseload, track the number of cases signed up, rejected or settled, measure how quickly cases are moving towards resolution, establish an average time from sign-up to settlement: The options are limitless. Within each metric, I have filters to drill down the numbers to some very specific and helpful statistics regarding efficiencies or inefficiencies. Performance can be measured with creative analytics.

In my practice, where the attorneys don't bill their time, it's harder to ascertain their true value to the firm. With billable practices, it's easier to measure performance and set goals: Just tie everything to the number of hours billed. That tells you exactly how much money that associate brought to the firm. For a contingency business, it's not so easy.

Financial data abounds with the right programs and metrics. There are tons of bookkeeping and financial programs with phenomenal reporting capabilities. Even case management software can provide useful money information. I track all kinds of financials: income from each of my referral sources; expense reports for budgeting; and the list goes on.

My advice: Legal technology can be complex because it changes all the time, and because lawyers were never taught technology strategy in law school. You need to adopt the right tools and keep up with trends. Being curious and open to change enables you to run an efficient and effective practice, choose the right solutions from the slew available, and make the technology work for you, not against you.

KNOWLEDGE IS POWER

I love technology! It's differentiates the young from the old! And I don't mean that in terms of age, but in terms of advancement. Technology advances us as people and as a society. There is no way to ignore technology and keep up in business. You don't need to know all the latest and greatest but certainly you must keep up!

I have a profound love and appreciation for technology. Years ago, while attending Adelphi University for my MBA, I had to create and deliver a presentation about the negative aspects of technology. I remember that I just couldn't do it. I didn't believe it and refused to try to convince my class of any negativity about anything. It just wasn't in my DNA. What did I do? The opposite.

My opening line was, "Never let anyone tell you that you can't change the world (insert quiet, dramatic pause here) because Mark Zuckerberg DID!" (Insert mic drop here ... HA!). I then discussed all the amazing ways Facebook created a communication forum for people all over the world. Although Myspace existed before, it was Facebook at the forefront of social media, created by a student, who had no clue of the impact or bigness of his idea! That itself is amazing to me!

Needless to say, even though I totally dismissed the topic I was given (surprising ... HA!), I did get an A on that presentation and in that class. I did also end up taking a "permanent leave" the following semester. Just as I am teaching you to follow your heart and your dreams, I didn't love spending my time OR money learning about things I had no interest in. It just didn't make any sense to me. I had already started my coaching business and to spend one minute of my life NOT loving it wasn't worth it to me. And it hasn't been worth it since. BUT I still remember that day and appreciate all that technology has offered me … including Facebook!

Google

LOVE HER. Whether I'm shopping for specific pair of oxford shoes or confirming that I used a word correctly, I LOVE HER. USE HER. FOR EVERYTHING.

Social Media

This one is super simple. It's called FREEEEEEEE ADVERTISING. Most small businesses don't maximize this as much as they should, which is why that's good for you. Social media is an amazing platform to connect with people, a.k.a. your future clients. It's a way to offer value, market yourself, and build a community.

Getting the word out about your business, successes, news, whatever, and all in a platform that reaches potentially millions of people across the globe, for free. How can you NOT take advantage of that?

We've already discussed the details of how to maximize social media (and Jeff explains more in the next chapter). The message here is: Don't just *embrace* technology, LOVE IT. All of it. Don't be a dinosaur. Be open to it. Don't be scared. Don't be resistant. Don't be dismissive of it. It's here, it's the future, and it's all good!

YouTube

I LOVE YouTube. You should too!

Seriously, what a concept! Search any question and find countless videos providing answers. What's better than that? Business questions, technical questions, personal questions, silly questions, dumb questions or just out of curiosity questions – they're all there. Use this tool. It's FREE information and it should become your very BEST FRIEND. Knowledge is power, and

YOUTUBE is filled with it! Remember, this is your life and your business. Empower yourself with as much knowledge as possible.

Back in the day, when I first started my business and hired someone to create my business website, I was totally overcharged, and the process is a bad memory. BUT, like everything in life, it "encouraged" (a.k.a. forced) me to learn about websites so I wouldn't be clueless to the process and rely on someone to update, maintain … blah, blah … especially since a website is critical to my business. So, one thousand YouTube videos later and counting (ha), in the past 10 years I have built 10 different websites for my business on my own. Plus, when I do farm out work, I know what's required. I'm clear about what the price range and time requirements should be.

BIG TIP: You see, knowledge is power, and that bad experience actually benefitted me and encouraged me to learn something I probably would not have, which in turn has saved me lots of time and money. This is a perfect example of how when something doesn't go as planned, don't freak out or become frustrated. Instead, think about how you can benefit from the situation. I had no clue how valuable website skills and tools would be to the overall success of my business. That's also a great example of going with the flow and embracing things as they come. It shows how to use a negative experience as motivation, not as a deterrent.

EXTRA TIP: Think of YouTube as a digital TV to showcase your own talents and advertise your business. Create your own YouTube channel educating people about legal issues. Use it to answer questions about how and when to seek legal advice. In the end, mention your own legal services. This promotes your brand and can certainly bring in more clients.

JEFF CHAPTER ELEVEN

ADVERTISING

As a solo or small business owner, you must advertise. Did you hear that? You HAVE TO advertise! What's that you say? How can you afford that 30-second Super Bowl commercial? You don't even have the budget for the 2:30 a.m. slot on the home shopping network? Despise the thought of having your name on a billboard? No money to produce and pay for a radio spot?

I get it. Listen, you've gotten this far in this book. You know the numbers. You have a budget. But that's not what I'm talking about. Put away the profit/loss sheet for a second. This is important. Even though it's almost the last chapter, it's important!

The Business Is You

You are *always* advertising your business. Always! Every minute of every day. As a solo or small business owner, the business is YOU. Even if you're on the train right now reading (or listening to) this book, you're advertising. The person sitting next to you sees you with a book about running a business and being mindful of your mental health and well-being. That says something about you! You're surely dressed appropriately and look the part of a successful lawyer heading to the office. An impression of you is forming in that person's mind.

Consciously or unconsciously, that person's brain comes to some conclusion or opinion about you. If you were dressed in a military uniform, sitting with your arms folded, just staring straight ahead, the person's impression is different. If you were wearing ripped jeans and a sweatshirt playing a video game on your phone, that creates another impression. If you speak loudly on your phone about how great your date was last night, so loudly that everyone on the train could hear, that's a whole other impression.

You get it? It's all about you. The way you carry yourself. The confidence you convey. The professionalism you display. The energy you radiate. All that matters. People see and feel that. You're always advertising you being you. And if you listen to Connie and you're happy and confident being you, and you live your life that way in the office, at home and everywhere else, people notice and are attracted to that. When they need a lawyer, they'll think of you.

You never know where your next case comes from. It may be that person your cousin brings to Thanksgiving dinner or the parent of your child's classmate you meet at parent-teacher conference night or the person selling you a new pair of shoes. In all these settings, you are your own walking advertisement. Therefore, you must always be cognizant of your appearance, your demeanor, and your conduct. You're always "on."

Please don't take all this the wrong way. It's not meant to scare you or change you or make you someone you're not. You shouldn't consciously make an "effort" in each of these circumstances. What I'm saying (and what Connie would say) is this: Just be you.

As someone running a business or striving to be a business owner, you already have that confidence in yourself. If you didn't, you wouldn't want to be the boss. Find that person you're most happy being and be that person all the time. Don't change who you are at Thanksgiving dinner or at the parent-teacher conference or in the shoe store. Know your comfort zone and own it. Don't change who you are to please anyone.

My message is this: Stay true to who you are to please *yourself*. That's the ticket! When you're happy and confident in yourself, that's attractive. People naturally notice and become drawn to that. Deep down, everyone wants that; they just don't realize it. When you've got it and you show it, that's more valuable and effective than the best advertising you can buy.

Here's the best part of all this: How much does it cost? Nothing. That surely fits in your budget. It's a mindset, an attitude, and a way of life, all of which are priceless.

Social Media

What else is free? Social media. F-R-E-E, people! How many people worldwide use social media? Care to guess? How about over 3 billion! That's billion, with a "b". More than two-thirds of American adults use Facebook regularly. The average person spends 2 hours and 22 minutes on social media *per day*!

If your business does not have a presence on social media, you might as well be invisible. I used to think that nobody looks for lawyers on-line. I was wrong. Today's legal consumers are changing the way they make decisions. Just like people trying to diagnose their own illnesses instead of (or in addition to) seeing a doctor, they are more engaged in choosing an attorney.

If you're a Millennial or younger, you probably know this. If you're a Gen-Xer or older, you're aware of it, but you must accept it. This is what people do now: Whether it's first thing in the morning, last thing before bed, any time they can sneak a peek at their desks or all the above, they're online. They need to know: Has anyone texted me? What's the latest news? Quick weather check? Any new posts on FB or LinkedIn? Did someone just visit my front door? Is the dog ok? (The last 2 were home security cameras check-ins!).

Google

Google yourself. Try it right now, I'll wait.

What came up? What if a potential client Googled you and saw those results? Would that person be impressed? Intrigued? Disappointed? Confused? This is important!

Everyone Googles everyone and everything now! Including me! I can't count how many times a day I Google things. At almost every lunch conversation in the office, something comes up that someone must Google. Whether it's fact-checking someone's claim that Taylor Swift is 31 years old, how many movies Kevin Bacon's been in, last night's Knicks game score, tomorrow's weather, or Bill Gates' net worth, it's utterly endless.

Google is a verb now. It's what people do. If you Google your name and nothing comes up you've got to change that. Ideally, a Google search will reveal your firm's website, Facebook page, LinkedIn page, contact information, maybe an article you've published, a flattering image of you, whatever. Something's got to come up!

Consumers are either searching for lawyers on the internet or confirming that the lawyer someone referred "checks out." Almost everyone referred to me has Googled my name and my firm's name before they call or visit my office. Either way, my internet and social media presence matter. Those things certainly influence people's decisions.

Your website and social media are often the first impression for potential clients, even before they call or see you. That means they've already begun forming opinions about you and your firm. For all you know, you may have already lost clients who couldn't find you online or weren't impressed with your website or Facebook page. Not having a website or social media presence these days says something; usually something negative.

I'm not trying to scare you. But this is real. And I'm not suggesting a complete internet overhaul for you and your firm in one week. It's a process. There's so much you can do. It's easy. Take it step by step. All these platforms are easy to set up and manage. If you're personally intimidated, get over it! Or just have someone (younger) help you. Start with a good photo, spend some time creating a bio (explaining what you do and why you're great at it) and start posting some photos and interesting things about your firm and your accomplishments.

I learn so much these days from YouTube. There are instructional videos about everything, even social media. Just go to YouTube and search "set up Facebook page" or "set up LinkedIn account" and you'll find tons of videos with step by step instructions. If you open your mind, take a deep breath, and set aside some time, it's easy.

Website

I started this discussion with social media, but that was partly to just get your attention. Your website is really the first step. That's your home. That's where you want potential clients to check you out. Browsing your site is akin to a personal office meeting. People see what you look like and what your office looks like (photos are important!). Thoughtful content provides in-depth information about you and your staff. Your firm's history and attorney bios tell a story. Prior successes (testimonials) resonate with people. Impressive past results influence others. Your contact information, by email, phone, or snail mail must be prominent. Make it easy for them to reach you.

The interaction between social media and your website is important. The purpose of a social media presence is to be noticed, celebrate your firm, and promote your brand. But the goal is to get customers inside the store! Everything you post should bring them onto your website.

Without getting too advanced on the social media details, it's important to "link" whatever you're posting to your website. Think of window-shopping: As you walk along Fifth Avenue in Manhattan, the window displays get you into the store. That's what social media does. But your social media provides the door; that's what the link is. It's something they "click" on, which then brings them directly to your website. Once they're on your website (and in the store), they're likely to start browsing around, like you do at Macy's or Bloomingdales. You want them in the store. You want them to browse. You want them to like what they see. And you want them to buy your stuff.

Websites reflect your business and your brand. Some websites are loaded with "calls to action." Those are sites where bells, whistles and pop-ups jump out periodically, telling the viewer to "call now" or "don't wait;" phone numbers flash across the screen; mini "chat boxes" appear allowing real-time messaging with a hired service.

All those are certainly effective for the right business model or brand. Other websites (like mine) are more informative and subtle. Currently, people already referred to me primarily view my website. They visit the site to check me out and gain more information on who we are. It's not built to get business as much as it's built to inform, enhance, and solidify our brand. However, that may change soon.

Years ago, just as we launched our first website, we also created a firm brochure. It was a beautiful, tasteful, glossy booklet with professional photos and content. After signing up a new case, we wanted clients to physically take something home. Nowadays, the internet covers that. We provide custom printed folders for clients to organize documents from the intake (much cheaper than brochures), but our website now replaces the brochure.

Keep in mind that website technology and styles change rapidly. My website gets a "facelift" every few years. Be open to that and accept it. Don't get frustrated spending money on a website upgrade. It needs to happen eventually so budget for it. It's money well spent.

Creative Advertising

Print advertising still works. In the right publication, an ad for law services may do very well. But that costs money. There is a way to appear in print without having to pay. Have you ever read the Law Journal (I hope so)? You've seen the columns and special feature sections such as "Outside Counsel." Guess what? The Law Journal and other publications happily accept articles from regular attorneys, like you, on current topics in the law. They're often starving for content! What better way to be published than to write an article for the Law Journal? It doesn't cost anything. Even better, when your article is published, your picture and bio are featured, along with your firm's name. What's better press than that? Suddenly, you're an authority on something!

I stumbled into this before I became a partner in my firm. Deep into a medical malpractice case just before trial, my adversary questioned my expert's opinions, claiming they weren't based on generally accepted scientific principles and not supported by relevant medical literature and studies. He moved to preclude my expert from testifying, which would have ended the case. This forced a hearing (called a *Frye* hearing in New York) where my expert had to testify and justify his opinions. Of course, motion papers submitted by each side preceded the hearing. I won the hearing and the case soon settled.

My boss was thrilled with the result and he noted how much effort went into my motion papers. The *Frye* issue was big at the time; courts were differing on whether it was appropriate to entertain such motions in medical malpractice cases. "You did all that research and wrote a great brief," he told me, "why don't you turn that into an article for the Law Journal?"

It was brilliant advice! I just tweaked my motion papers a bit. Instead of arguing one side, I presented a more fair and balanced analysis (of course concluding that the plaintiff's side was more persuasive). The Law Journal accepted it and published it, along with my photo and bio. What's more, it was such a hot topic that a few months later a trial judge faced with a *Frye* issue wrote a decision in favor of the plaintiff and cited my article as support! I was referenced in a published court decision! That's advertising you can't buy even if you wanted to. Pretty cool stuff.

Traditional Advertising

Old school advertising methods are far from dead. They've just changed a bit. Nobody searches through phone books and yellow pages, but you still can pay to have your name, or your firm seen. Buying advertising is simple on Google or other search engines. Just set a goal (more views on the website or calls to the office), decide on the target audience (one county, all five boroughs, multiple states; the sky is the limit!), create your message and decide how much you want spend. These search engines are much more efficient at targeting a very specific audience. Their algorithms can track what people do, what they search, what they buy, etc. Sometimes I feel like they can read my mind. All I need to do is think about my next vacation, and ads for beautiful destinations and great deals start popping up on my Facebook feed and Google searches!

My firm uses a combination of traditional-like methods and social media. The biggest advertising decision I made was hiring a Public Relations consultant. Budgeting for that position was worth it. I could spend that money on TV commercials, billboards, and Google ads, but those mediums aren't consistent with the message I want to send to potential clients about my firm.

Also, we get most of our business from attorneys who refer personal injury and medical malpractices. That's a very specific audience. Their incentive is a percentage of the fee when the case resolves. That's been our main source of business for years, but given the acceptance and ease of online tools, we now target the general public in an "under the radar" type of way.

How? Instead of the stereotypical commercial with a paid actor questioning if you're hurt and providing a 1-800 number (which does work, by the way), we built a social media and internet platform to spread the word about our successes and charitable work. Connecting our posts, photos and messages through Facebook, LinkedIn and our website, we get people's attention, boast a bit of our accomplishments, and then direct them to our website, where they can really see and read what we're about. Many of our referring attorneys are my Facebook "friends" and "follow" my firm on Facebook and LinkedIn; as do many non-lawyers, friends, and family of the attorneys and staff and anyone else interested in the stuff we post.

Hiring A Consultant

My PR consultant took all this to a new level. She provides tremendous skill and insight into creating posts with beautiful imaging, professional quality, and effective messages, all working to promote our brand. We updated our overall color scheme and firm logo, as well. It's all about branding, people! She introduced us to programs that schedule posts to appear on social media platforms automatically on a daily, weekly, monthly (or whatever) basis. It's not that hard!

We upgraded our website to interact seamlessly with the online stuff. The news, successes, stories, and announcements we post succinctly on Facebook and LinkedIn all have links to direct the user to our website, where the full story is explained with more facts, details, and photos. Once someone is on our site, it's easy to navigate to our attorney bios, successes, firm history, photos, etc. to really get to know us. All this is no different from that retail clothing store having a great window display to draw customers in, organizing the store strategically for people to see what's for sale, employing good salespeople to sell the products, getting people to try some stuff on until they find what fits and then buying the product!

As lawyers, we're selling a service, but the idea and methodology are the same. People have choices. New York has more lawyers per person than any other state. Therefore, New Yorkers have lots of choices! What sets you apart? What makes you different? Why should someone choose your firm? Your website and social media postings should answer those questions.

I always tell clients that when they hire my firm, we're entering into a long-term relationship. We have to really like each other, trust each other, believe in each other, and communicate well with each other. Many of our cases take years to resolve, so there's plenty of interaction between them and us. Our website and social media posts often set the tone for the relationship. Why? Because our clients usually see and experience those before they come to the office and meet us. Remember what I said about first impressions!

Existing and Former Clients

Another market we target: existing and former clients. My firm has been in business for 35 years. We've helped thousands of people. Many of these people refer family and friends in need of our help. Those are the most valuable cases to me since I don't have to share the legal fee with a referring attorney. That's a full 1/3 more for me! I love my referring attorneys, but I am paid a lot more without them.

Targeting our existing and former client base with our "under the radar" approach increases the "direct cases" we get. How? Email, for one. Everyone has email. All email addresses are collected at intake. Make sure everyone who enters those addresses does so consistently in the software program! Put them all in the same box! That way, they can easily be harvested for email blasts. It's easy to hire a service to create, manage and provide stats on email blasts.

We also do quarterly newsletters. Those are issued electronically (by email) and by hard copy (snail mail). Sure, there's a cost, but it's another way to "touch" these people and remind them of what we do. We limit the hard copy newsletters to only referring attorneys. This keeps the cost down. What else? We periodically provide public service announcements (like explaining SUM and UM insurance benefits, tips on what to do after a car accident, education on new laws passed, etc.). These are done by email, social media posts, or regular mail.

Your client base is a great source of potential business. They already used your services! If you buy a toothpaste and you love it, don't you buy it again? When you have a great experience at the Gap buying clothes, don't you return the next time you shop? It's almost criminal for you NOT to exploit this asset. And it feels good to help someone a second time. It reaffirms the commitment to the relationship you built. Everyone in the firm loves when a client returns (most of the time!). Allocating a part of your budget to remain in contact with these people is a must!

My advice: More and more people go online for goods, services, advice, and every other resource imaginable. I'm not yet convinced that most people *begin* their search for a lawyer online (many surely do), but once they find one, you can bet they'll check out the firm's website and social media presence. Work on those now!

YOU ARE THE BRAND

Jeff makes some great points on this. All that website and social media stuff is hugely important. But I want to (again) stress what's most important in advertising: YOU. You advertise yourself.

As a business owner, your personal life and business life must be the same. You can't have happiness and success in one and not the other. You are your business. There is no beginning and end to your day. And when you begin to love life and your business, things will start to mesh in a very different, enjoyable way.

REAL sustainable success comes with loving your business AND your life. If one lacks, they both do. You want both and you can have both, but you must look at both as one and the same because that's what they are. They are the total of you.

It's All About You

Don't ever forget: *You are the brand.* That's right. You're not just another one of those countless lawyers out there. You are your own personal brand (btw, this goes for any profession). Which means, and I don't want to scare you, that you are a SALESPERSON. That's right. I said it. In fact, every single person in all professions are salespeople. Deal with it! Once you do, and understand what that means, you will see your life AND business turn around quickly! For some reason, some people have this awful view of sales, but those people are clueless, and I'll tell you why.

To be a great lawyer, people must *like* you before they hire you. Your skillset does not matter if you can't get the business. Therefore, you must master the art of sales and it's not what you think. It doesn't entail boring networking meetings or torturing yourself with an elevator speech. It's much easier than that.

I call it the art of "being you." Can you imagine? I know, you can't. But that's how simple it is: It's being clear about who you are and what you stand for. Not who you think you should be. It's showing up every day being your unique, incredible, confident self. Because that sets you apart from all other lawyers. There's only one YOU. And when you embrace YOU, you show up in business and life very differently.

You see, you can have it all. A successful business and a fun, enjoyable life. How? It requires you to be open to thinking differently. Your mindset dictates everything: successes and failures. You control the outcome by how you think. Isn't that worth learning? To think on purpose. That's what I teach: purposeful, powerful, and positive thinking.

How do I do it? Each morning, I remind myself who I am. I write a list of all my positive qualities and attributes. Yes, I actually write them down on paper. It's my daily routine: Wake up, brush my teeth, make coffee, grab my pad and a pen, and start making my lists. The lists are about me. What I appreciate about MYSELF and what makes ME unique.

What does this do? It keeps me clear on who I am and focused on my positive qualities (everyone has them!). This practice sets the proper tone for my mindset each day, which in turn sets the right tone for my day. The best part: It never matters what happened yesterday, last year or last night. Each day brings the power to make a difference. *Loving and appreciating yourself gives YOU the power to do it.*

Jeff Chapter Twelve

FINAL THOUGHTS

Congratulations, people! You made it to my final chapter. I'm sure ideas are buzzing around your brains. I feel your excitement and anticipation as you consider your new business strategies. It's a great feeling! What do you take on first? Networking, advertising, hiring, or budgeting? There's no right answer; only what's good for you and your business.

Whatever your decisions are, you should be proud of yourself for taking the step of reading this book (or some other book like this), doing something to take control of your life, being proactive in pursuing a goal, thinking outside the box and being true to yourself. From this moment on, every decision you make is the right one! Even if something doesn't work out, it will be a learning experience from which you will certainly grow. Everything happens for a reason. There's a reason you read this book! Find the positives in all that happens in your business and in life and be amazed at how successes and happiness will follow!

Here are some final tidbits to help you focus and maintain success.

Attend CLE Lectures

We didn't talk much about the law in this book. Don't forget you're still a lawyer! Running the business is important but keeping current with changes in the law and getting out of the office is important, too. You need the CLE credits, anyway. You could take the easy way out and do an online course at home in your pajamas, but I like the real thing.

As a young attorney, I attended as many lectures as I possibly could. My goal was to take at least one piece of useful information from each one. For every lecture hour, if I gained some kernel of good advice, it was worth it. And it's a social thing. You meet people, network, relax, and maybe learn something. I generally chose the course by the speaker. If it were someone interesting and dynamic, I'd go. The programs can be as entertaining as educational.

These days I lecture much more than I attend. If that's something you're into, go for it! I find it fun and extremely rewarding. I lecture on business related stuff just as much as law stuff. I'm fortunate to have attorneys covering the work back at the office, but even if you're a solo, making the time to be a lecturer is worth it. For your business, it's a terrific way to market and build your brand. Once you lecture, you're an authority! Whether 10 or 100 people attend, publicizing your participation as a speaker and posting some pictures of you behind the podium sends the message. Of course, that kind of public speaking is not for everyone, but if you can swing it, go for it.

Organize

Organization is a personal thing. It means different things to different people. I'm pretty neat. To me, organization means my desktop is clean. Maybe a few Post-it Notes by my phone but leaving the office with a clean desk is my goal every day. It doesn't always happen, but I try.

That's not everyone. Years ago, I hired a *per diem* appellate attorney for appeals and heavy motions. He worked in the building next to mine, so I just walked over when an issue arose. The man was (and is) a genius. He's a walking encyclopedia of caselaw. He knows the cases *and the exact citations* off the top of his head. I kid you not! His mind works like an organized Amazon warehouse!

But his office? His floor and desktop resemble the New York City skyline. Piles of papers stacked to different heights everywhere. Some teeter dangerously close to toppling. Walking through this is like traversing a minefield. Each pile is an appeal or motion in progress. To me, it looks like a complete mess! I sweat just thinking about it. Nevertheless, this guy knows each matter associated with every stack. This is his filing system! It suits the way his brain works. The Smith case? That's over there in the corner. Jones? Second pile from the left on the couch. He doesn't hesitate. I wouldn't be able to function. The clutter would drive me nuts!

Being organized helps me focus. When I'm preparing for trial or considering a structural change in the organization, I need a method. We have about 50 total employees. Every so often, an attorney leaves or a new one is hired. Our organizational structure is comprised of teams, each led by an attorney who oversees 3-6 staff members. So, when a new attorney comes aboard, we need to re-evaluate the teams. If we need to shuffle things around, it can get complicated. I use a poster-board and post-its. Putting everyone's name on a post-it and sticking it on the board gives me the visual I need. I separate the teams in chart form and just stare at it. I ask my partners and managers for input. It's easy to just move the post-its around and create different team combinations. Most importantly, it works for me!

You do what works for you.

Prioritize

As your business grows and you take on more work, it's easy to get lost in the minutia. There's always something you can do on every case and there's always some part of the business to focus on. Every minute, you make decisions about what to do next. How do you choose? It's so tempting to keep choosing easy tasks to perform, but the difficult, tough, annoying, time-consuming stuff needs to get done, too!

I know, you put off calling Mrs. Jones to reject her case. You know she's going to fight you about it and you're not in the mood to fight. I know, that discovery motion needs to be done, but you need to research some key points and you can't bear the thought of doing that. I know, you have those medical records to review, but with a 1,500-page hospital chart, you don't know where to start. I know, you've been meaning to scrutinize your monthly bills to see where you can save money, but you keep pushing that off for next month.

Here's my mantra, people: DO IT NOW! A law school professor of mine gave that advice. As a young associate at a law firm, he made a sign with that phrase and taped it above the doorframe in his office. Every time he looked toward that door, he saw it. Every time his mind wandered and drifted toward procrastination, he read it. I've had that same sign hanging in my office for 25 years.

It's tempting to just check off the easy stuff every day. It keeps you busy but lulls you into a false sense of security. One meaningful task is often worth more than ten menial ones. Act purposefully. Don't just react to every question and every task that arises. Pick and choose how you spend your time. Make it your business to tackle the difficult tasks, especially if those will move the business forward.

Know yourself and your habits. If you're a morning person, get in early and do the important things first. If you're a night person, do the easy things early and save the cerebral tasks for later. Be honest with yourself and understand your strengths and weaknesses.

Avoid being sucked into rabbit holes! It's easy to get distracted while completing a difficult task. When writing a motion, legal research online easily takes you from one case on point to another to another and so on. You spend all day clicking from case to case. You end up with additional knowledge on some topic, but did that help you finish the motion?

Additional issues pop up with every task. I make money transfers online from the escrow account into the operating account. If my task is to make one or two transfers, I often get sucked in to viewing all the balances in the account. I'm already there, so why not? Before I know it, I'm scanning through last month's checks, looking for irregularities. Then I'm analyzing my line of credit and seeing if the interest rates have changed. These may be worthwhile tasks, but that isn't why I went online. If I otherwise planned to return some important phone calls after making the simple transfer, I get distracted! Stay focused and do what needs to be done.

Delegate

You can't do everything. As the business grows, invest the time to find the right people to take on your journey. Finding the right person can make a world of difference to you and your firm. Be selective in the hiring process and don't be afraid to dole out responsibility.

Often, it's the first step that's the hardest. A solo practitioner making all the decisions and doing all the work may not trust anyone. It's true: Nobody will care as much about the cases and about the business as you. But in order to grow, you must get passed that. Finding responsible, hardworking, reliable people will help you grow and keep you sane.

The goal is to make money, I get it. But it's also to be happy. You can make money alone, but the idea of hiring people, creating a work environment that suits you and your needs, and then molding, teaching and shaping people to all work together, get along and achieve common goals is equally rewarding.

As the boss, you really affect people's lives. You set the tone for the office culture. Most people spend more time in the office than at home with their families. That's a big deal! Delegating responsibilities to these people and watching them grow and thrive as employees and as people is really what this is all about. Embrace it.

Acknowledge Referrers

Whatever your source of business, attorneys, former clients, friends, family, or associates, you must graciously acknowledge their efforts. Even if you don't accept the case, express your gratitude in some way. Every encounter with a referrer, whether by phone, letter, email, or text is meaningful.

Marketing people talk about "touches." Each act to reach out and "touch" a potential business source counts for something. It's true! I can't tell you how often I call a referring attorney for some reason (to report the status of a case; to ask advice; or to just say hi), and that attorney says, "Oh, I'm so glad you called; this case has been on my desk for two weeks and I've been meaning to refer it to you." This really happens!

As a simple advertising concept, the more someone sees and hears about something, the more likely they'll remember it. If the McDonald's commercial comes on five times during the first half of the football game, more people are likely to get a Big Mac at halftime! I don't think of my referrers as "customers" to buy my product, but the concept is similar. I am truly appreciative that these people think of me, trust me, and believe in me enough to refer me work. I cherish and nurture these relationships. I genuinely like these people. I may not socialize with all of them on the weekends, but I make sure they know how much I appreciate their business.

Dress For Success

Here's a subject constantly evolving. We've gone from suits all the time, to casual Fridays, to business casual all the time, to now sort of back to suits, but still very casual. What's the deal?

While appearance isn't everything, it certainly counts. Most people expect their lawyers to look like lawyers. But these days, what does that mean? For me, it's either formal business attire or business casual. If I'm going to court, of course it's formal. I used to tell my associates they had three choices for court: 1) blue suit, white shirt, blue tie; or 2) blue suit, white shirt, blue tie; or 3) blue suit, white shirt, blue tie. Of course, I'm exaggerating; I didn't care if they wore a red tie ☺. But things have changed. Judges are younger and much more tolerant and current on fashion. That doesn't mean courts have gone casual! You still wear suits to court.

In the office, I'm almost always business casual, unless I have a client appointment or meeting scheduled. That's why I have a few "emergency suits" hanging in the closet. Full outfits, including socks and shoes, await the "pop in" client who wasn't scheduled or the call to meet a potential new client immediately. Those suits have been used on many occasions. My casual attire skips the tie but usually includes a dress shirt and sports jacket. I'll also go with sweaters and vests in the colder weather. Shoes are trickier. I mostly wear the leather dress shoes, but have some more casual ones, too. People are getting very ambitious with socks these days; they seem to be where lawyers make their fashion statements.

Female lawyers – you're pretty much on your own here. This is a good example of knowing what you don't know and not saying much. Just make sure skirts are not too short.

Return Phone Calls

What's the most frequent complaint made by clients to the Bar Association? "My lawyer doesn't return my phone calls." I know you're busy. The last thing you want to do is call back that annoying, pesky client and listen to a 30-minute rant. But you must call. You're his lawyer. Who knows, maybe he's calling to refer a case.

My firm's policy is that client phone calls must be returned the same day. If the call is after hours, it must be returned the next day. Are there exceptions? Of course. But train everyone to get in the habit of returning calls promptly. Your clients are waiting to hear from you.

Take Care Of YOU

Vacations aren't a luxury. They are necessary for a well-balanced, healthy life. You must take time off. You need to reset your brain. You must enjoy life (just ask Connie!). You need to spend alone time with your partner (if you have one). You need to spend quality time with yourself. Taking time away from work has physical and psychological benefits – there are studies on this, people. It's proven!

Vacations reduce stress, motivate you, and improve your outlook on life. There's more to life than work! You work hard to enjoy life. I enjoy my life at work, but I also look forward to traveling the world, seeing cool places, doing fun things, and meeting new people (outside of a business setting). The experiences I share with Connie (and our dog Pumkin) outside the office are the ones I cherish most. During the holidays, when I reflect on the past year, I'm more grateful and appreciative of the vacations we've taken and time we've spent together outside the office than anything else.

Work is important. Running a business can be fun. But let's keep our perspective, people! Life's about being happy. So, Start Loving Life in the office and everywhere else!!!

Connie Chapter Twelve

YOU CONTROL YOUR OWN DESTINY

Your last chapter! You have learned to be YOU at all times, under all circumstances. So, let's wrap it all up.

You control your own destiny. That's not a question, it's a fact. Believe it. Once you embrace this, you will approach your career and life differently. You see, you can have any life you want.

But you first must be clear on this question: What does your ideal life look like for you? There is no wrong or right answer. Your answer will evolve over time. The most important thing is to first create the vision of what you want. You may have already heard this, but it's worth repeating: You must start with the end in mind. It will keep you motivated.

Your end goal is not based on what you have lived or what you "think" you can achieve. It's the opposite. *It is about what you "want" to achieve, without being limited by the past.* So many people insist on being *realistic* about what's possible for them. That mindset limits you.

My philosophy is about thinking bigger and knowing that whatever you want is possible. And not letting your current reality hold you back. Your current reality is already old news. You are living it. And you are living it based on the limited mindset to which you are accustomed. Now it's about creating a new mindset and vision for your future, because once you do anything is possible. You just need to remind yourself, each and every day.

Are you in love with you? I know that sounds super-cheesy and, knowing most lawyers, I can virtually see many eye-rolls out there. But those eye-rollers are the lawyers whose confidence is shaped by accolades. The problem with this mindset is that you can't always have wins (at trial or anywhere else). It's not possible! Don't let your life and your confidence be shaped by such unattainable external conditions or expectations.

Mainstream society wants it to be this: Winning feels great; losing feels crappy. I don't know about you, but to me this sounds like torture and pressure to always be winning. It's not ideal and, in fact, impossible to achieve. That mindset puts you under constant, undue pressure to feel only as good as your last win. It's fleeting and not productive at all. Don't think that way.

You want and deserve a life where you feel good most of the time. *Your life should be measured not by your "wins" but by you being YOU.* Sure, winning feels good. But not winning is good, too. There's always something positive that comes from a loss. Disappointments happen for a reason. They are teachable moments. They prepare us for the next endeavor. Every closed door leads to an open one. You just have to pull the next door with confidence. Believe that!

Sometimes you're not supposed to win a trial. Sometimes your client really doesn't deserve to win. Sometimes the facts just aren't on your side. Sometimes you lose a client and it's a blessing. Sometimes you don't get the case, but it's really a godsend. Sometimes someone quits, and it's a good thing for everyone. Let things flow in a systematic way instead of being harsh on yourself. If you're not able to achieve something, no problem. That will be your chance to really choose what's best for YOU. If you have a hard time doing that, shoot me a text 😊!

YOU matter most. When you realize and accept this, your life will be much easier, things will start falling into place, and eventually success will come. But you must believe in YOU and do what feels right to YOU.

Sometimes a pandemic hits the world, but it allows you to reset the vision of your firm and your future. Everything life offers has value. Put your mind in a position to see it.

That's how you Start Loving Life!!!

LET'S CONNECT

For more information on Jeff's law firm, go to www.sskblaw.com.

Check out Connie's life coaching practice websites:
www.startlovinglife.com, www.conniehenriquez.com and
www.startlovinglifeforlawyers.com.

Follow Connie on Instagram at @startlovinglifenow and subscribe to her
YouTube channel *Start Loving Life®️ with Connie*.

Watch Connie and Jeff lecturing for *Lawline* in New York at
https://www.lawline.com/course/client-intake-in-personal-injury-cases-in-
new-york.

Lightning Source UK Ltd.
Milton Keynes UK
UKHW022017241120
374038UK00015B/487/J